THE NEXT-TO-LAST WORD

THE NEXT-TO-LAST WORD

Service, Hope, and Revival
in the Postexilic Prophets

Michael P. V. Barrett

Grand Rapids, Michigan

Reformation Heritage Books
2965 Leonard St. NE
Grand Rapids, MI 49525
616–977–0889 / Fax 616–285–3246
orders@heritagebooks.org
www.heritagebooks.org

Printed in the United States of America
15 16 17 18 19 20/10 9 8 7 6 5 4 3 2 1

Library of Congress Cataloging-in-Publication Data

Barrett, Michael P. V., 1949-
  The next-to-last word : service, hope, and revival in the postexilic prophets / Michael P. V. Barrett.
      pages cm
  Includes bibliographical references.
    ISBN 978-1-60178-427-8 (pbk. : alk. paper) 1. Bible. Zechariah—Criticism, interpretation, etc. 2. Bible. Haggai—Criticism, interpretation, etc. 3. Bible. Malachi—Criticism, interpretation, etc. I. Title.
  BS1665.52.B37 2015
  224'.906—dc23
                                        2015021404

For additional Reformed literature, request a free book list from Reformation Heritage Books at the above regular or e-mail address.

To Rev. Richard Eugene Crawford

More my brother than brother-in-law
and my lifelong friend

Ezra 1:

Contents

PART 4

Malachi: The Logician

Preface

I am not writing this little book for the academy. It is not intended to be a scholarly treatment. (Plenty of those types of books are available, and some are very good.) Therefore, I've not engaged in any interchange or conversation with other works and ideas, which is such a crucial part of scholarly writing but tends to be distracting to those in the wider audience who are not versed or expert in the technical jargon. I do make some references to a few other works, particularly some of my own and especially to the *Reformation Heritage KJV Study Bible*, which I had the privilege of working on. The thoughts that I expressed in my contributions to the Bible are the same as those I want to express here. Even when I feel it necessary to address critical or differing views from my own, I try to do it in a way that does not distract from the relevant message.

My passion in ministry both in the classroom and from the pulpit has been to open up the Old Testament Scripture to God's people—to take what on the surface seems to be complicated or obscure and to expound its message and demonstrate its relevance to life. In fact, much of what you will read in this book is adaptations of sermons I've preached over the years from these prophets. I can't help but introduce some grammatical terminology or refer to some literary devices in a few places, but I hope these discussions will not be intrusive. My concern is to sum up the messages of these three prophets and to point to the applications that address the same kind of issues in the modern church that existed in their postexilic congregations.

Admittedly, I'm responsible for the content, but I owe a word of thanks to many who have helped along the way. Not the least is my wife, Sandra, who has been, as with every other book I've written, the first to read every chapter as it is completed. She is sometimes too quick to say "nice job," but then returns the chapter to me with all the needed corrections circled.

I want to express my thanks as well to the staff of Reformation Heritage Books for all they have done in making the book a reality. Special thanks goes to Jay Collier for his prodding me to submit a manuscript and to Annette Gysen for her outstanding editorial work. Good editors are priceless. This is the first time we have worked together, but she knows how to make me sound like me—only better. I give my thanks to my boss, Joel Beeke, and Puritan Reformed Theological Seminary for including projects like this as part of my job description. Above all I thank the Lord for His amazing kindness in allowing me the privilege of sharing His Word with others. It is humbling.

—Michael P. V. Barrett

Introduction

Creed and custom often conflict. What is confessed to be truth does not always translate into practice. This is true for all too many Christians and regarding all too many aspects of Christian faith. Tragically, it is true at the most foundational level of Christianity, the Bible, which is the bedrock for faith. There is frequently a disconnect between what Christians believe about the Bible and what Christians do with the Bible. Orthodox theology declares that the Bible is the only rule for faith (what is to be believed) and practice (what is to be done). The Westminster Shorter Catechism explains that, apart from the Scripture, it is impossible to meet our chief end of glorifying and enjoying God: "The Word of God, which is contained in the Scriptures of the Old and New Testaments, is the only rule to direct us how we may glorify and enjoy him" (Q. 2). Even though they confess the importance of Scripture, Christians often relegate it to the fringes of life. Certainly conservative and confessing believers would be alarmed if Scripture reading and exposition were omitted from the liturgy of worship—and well they should be. Certainly evangelical Christians would be up in arms if the state confiscated personal copies of the Scriptures—and well they should be. But the trag-edy is that certain portions or even whole books of many of those personal copies could be excised surreptitiously, and many Christians would not miss them—and that would be a shame.

With some exceptions, the Old Testament suffers more from this neglect than the New. Some of the Old Testament narratives are well known and used frequently for moral lessons or warnings. Proverbs, with pithy advice touch-ing on life's situations, is a favorite of many, and blessing comes easily from the Psalms. But much of the Old Testa-ment is a closed book to so many. Admittedly, some surface issues account for this. How can something that was writ-ten so long ago to one group of people living in a relatively small bend of the globe address the needs and concerns of the modern world? Culture has changed; technology has advanced; the affairs of life must certainly be more com-plex. Some portions of the Old Testament seem to have no apparent value or purpose, such as the endless genealo-gies in Chronicles. Other passages seem to be completely outdated, such as the Levitical instructions concerning garments and grooming (Lev. 19:19, 27). Yet others appear to some to be outright offensive, such as the command to exterminate the Canaanites. The tension between the Old Testament's "then" and the current "now" has caused many, at least in practice, to adopt a hands-off policy regarding much of the Old Testament.

For various reasons, among the most ignored por-tions of the Old Testament are the Minor Prophets. Apart from Jonah's ordeal in the belly of the fish, some life-long churchgoers admit that they have never heard a sermon from the Minor Prophets, at least one that contextually and systematically deals with the particular prophet's unique message. Never hearing from the Minor Prophets from the pulpit increases the temptation to skip them in private reading and study as well. Consequently, the Minor Prophets remain virtually unknown. As a preacher, I always love to hear the rustling of Bible pages as the congregation turns to the text for exposition. However, there have been times when I've announced a text from the Minor Prophets, and the rustling goes on far too long. On occasion I've had to direct people to go to Matthew and then back up from there, or I have referred them to the table of contents. I've never had to do that when preaching from Romans.

Acknowledging the relevance of the Old Testament, including the Minor Prophets, to modern Christianity and life hinges on the full acceptance of 2 Timothy 3:16–17: "All scripture is given by inspiration of God, and is profitable for doctrine, for reproof, for correction, for instruction in righteousness: that the man of God may be perfect, thoroughly furnished unto all good works." That divinely inspired and infallible statement is all-inclusive regarding every book in the sacred canon, even the Minor Prophets. Of all the possible things the Lord could have said, He chose in His infinite wisdom to say what has been preserved for us in the Holy Scriptures. So rather than dismissing or ignoring these God-breathed-out words, every believer should approach the Scripture, including the Minor Prophets, with head and heart open to receive the profitable word.

Saying the message is relevant is one thing; discerning the message is another. How to discern and interpret the message is the question. Although the message of God's word is timelessly and universally relevant, it was nonetheless given at a point in time and to a particular people. The better we understand the historical circumstances, the better we can determine the significance of what God said then to extract the universal and timeless truth that applies to now. The application of a given truth may look different from time to time or from culture to culture, but truth is timelessly transcendent from any specific situation. So our not being physical descendants of Abraham living in the Middle East thousands of years ago does not diminish the relevance of the ancient message for modern man. The God of then, whether the then of the past or the future, is the God of now.

A key component of discovering the relevance of the Old Testament message to the church is to know something of Israel's history. It was a checkered history that moved through various stages: a huge extended family; a federation or confederation of tribes; a united monarchy; a divided monarchy; periods of exile and existence in the land under foreign sovereignty. Israel's national history began in the fifteenth century BC when the Lord redeemed the huge extended family of Abraham from Egyptian bondage and constituted them as a nation at Sinai. That initial federation or confederation of tribes ruled under theocracy and administered for a while under a series of judges transitioned to a united monarchy and then a divided monarchy with separate kingdoms in the north and south. The parallel kingdoms existed independently until the northern kingdom suffered exile under the Assyrians in the eighth century BC, and then the southern kingdom under the Babylonians in the sixth century BC. At every stage, the Lord had a message for His people. The time of the writing prophets, both Major and Minor, spanned the years of Israel's divided kingdoms through the northern and southern exiles into the period when some of Judah returned to the Promised Land, roughly from the ninth to the fifth centuries BC.

The focus of this study is on the period after the Babylonian exile. Throughout the Old Testament era, God had revealed His word faithfully and consistently, but now there were three final voices that would declare His word before a four-hundred-year period of silence: Haggai, Zechariah, and Malachi. These would not be years of divine inactivity, as providence orchestrated every event toward the fullness of time, but there would be no other prophetic voice until John the Baptist declared, "Behold the Lamb of God!" (John 1:36). John was able to point his finger quite literally to the One that every other prophet before him could only speak of "as they were moved by the Holy Ghost" (2 Peter 1:21). Although 1 and 2 Chronicles were the last books written in the Old Testament canon (finished in 425/4 BC, about ten years after Malachi), Haggai, Zechariah, and Malachi were the last of the old dispensation prophets. That God did not speak to another prophet for hundreds of years underscores the importance of what He said through these three. Last words are always important. Malachi prophesied that God would send His messenger to prepare the way

of the coming Christ (3:1), and all we have to do is turn
the page to the New Testament, in Matthew 3, to find that
messenger, John, in the process of preparing the way. The
Old Testament was not the last word after all, but its last
prophetic messages contribute significantly to our understanding of what God has spoken in these last days by His
Son (Heb. 1:2). The next-to-last word—written and spoken
by these postexilic prophets—sets the stage for hearing
God's final, ideal, and incomparable Word.

So in this little study, I want to consider the message
and theology of these postexilic prophets and their particular contributions and advancements of God's redemptive
message. They are ancient voices with a remarkably modern message. Understanding any communication requires
placing it in its proper context. In any conversation, mis-
interpretations are likely unless the whole conversation
is heard. This basic principle certainly applies to biblical
interpretation. Too often, readers of the Bible jump into
their reading at a particular point without factoring in what
had been said before or the contemporary circumstances
that were being addressed. Apart from the temporal and
circumstantial context, the prospect of misunderstanding
or not understanding increases. Consequently, I want to
approach this study in four parts. Part 1 will address just
the facts: facts about the prophetic office, facts about the
historical setting, and facts about the overall contribution
these three prophets make to God's overall redemptive
message. Parts 2–4 will then sum up the specific messages
of the prophets separately. Although Haggai, Zechariah,
and Malachi were equally inspired by the Holy Spirit and

shared the same agenda to set things in order for the coming of the Christ in the fullness of time, they were unique personalities with unique approaches. Haggai was a realist whose message was short, to the point, and at times not so sweet. Zechariah was an idealist whose encouraging message focused on the Lord's ultimate and climactic triumph over all wickedness and over every agency hostile to His purpose and kingdom. Malachi was a logician whose message relentlessly, irrefutably, and precisely identified the hindrances to spiritual life and revival, the obstacles to divine blessing.

Ultimately, my desire is to show the relevance of these three postexilic Minor Prophets to modern life. Their length qualifies them to be listed with the Minor Prophets, but their messages, like the nine others lumped in this category, are as major as it gets; they are just as inspired and authoritative as Isaiah, Jeremiah, and Ezekiel. Perhaps we should call them the Shorter Prophets to remove the stigma and the temptation to ignore them. When Paul, under inspiration, said that "all scripture is given by inspiration of God, and is profitable for doctrine, for reproof, for correction, for instruction in righteousness: that the man of God may be perfect, thoroughly furnished unto all good works" (2 Tim. 3:16–17), he included Haggai, Zechariah, and Malachi in that assessment. It is my prayer that the Holy Spirit will show this to be true in our experience as we reflect on this small portion of Scripture. If we find ourselves unable to see through the veil in the reading of the Old Testament, let us remember that the veil is "done away in Christ" (2 Cor. 3:14). It is all about Him, even the postexilic Minor Prophets.

I would encourage you as you read what I have to say about Haggai, Zechariah, and Malachi to have your Bible ready so you can read what they are saying. This will not be a verse-by-verse commentary, but this study will be based on the biblical text, and I will refer to specific references throughout. I don't suppose this book will fall into the category of casual reading, but I trust it will be simple and clear enough to provide a supplement to your personal Bible study. I would really recommend having at ready *The Reformation Heritage KJV Study Bible*. I had the privilege of editing the Old Testament and composing the notes for various books, including the Minor Prophets. Consequently, some of what I say here, particularly concerning basic facts about each book's dates, themes, and outlines, will parallel what I said there. The notes you find there will help you to see what I say here in the context of the actual text of Scripture.

QUESTIONS

1. Why does the Old Testament seem to be so difficult for many Bible readers? What portions give you the most difficulty?

2. Why is it important to know something about the historical context or setting of an Old Testament passage?

3. In what way are the postexilic prophets the next-to-last word? What is the last word?

4. What is a fundamental error Bible readers sometimes make in interpreting any portion of the Bible?

5. Why is the designation *Minor Prophets* misleading?

—PART 1—

Just the Facts

1

Facts about Their Job

Haggai, Zechariah, and Malachi are the last in a long line of Old Testament prophets. Prophets, along with priests and kings, held *messianic* positions, or jobs divinely established to serve God and His people. *Messiah* is the noun form of a Hebrew verb meaning "to spread a liquid over." The noun form conveys the passive idea of the verb: a messiah is one who has been anointed. The liquid most commonly used for anointing was olive oil, and it was smeared on both things and people. Most of the anointed objects were set apart for a distinct purpose and had some function in the ceremonies of worship rituals associated with the tabernacle or temple. The same significance applied to anointed people. The people anointed were usually in some civil or religious leadership capacity, the most common and significant categories being kings (e.g., 1 Kings 1:34), priests (e.g., Ex. 28:41), and prophets (e.g., 1 Kings 19:16). Anointing with oil was a symbolic gesture setting that person apart for a particular function. The Old Testament's frequent association of oil with the Holy Spirit is an important and significant component in the anointing ritual.

Any person anointed could be identified as a messiah, so kings, priests, and prophets were all messiahs. Being anointed marked a person as qualified and chosen to perform the task for which he was anointed. Messiahs had work to do: kings had to rule; priests had to minister; and prophets had to preach. Each of these lesser messiahs in his own way pointed to and prefigured the ideal Messiah, the perfect Prophet, Priest, and King together in one person, the Lord Jesus Christ. So by virtue of his office, not his person or performance, every prophet, priest, or king was a representative and foretaste of the Christ who came in the fullness of time. Zechariah said that the postexilic high priest Joshua and his attendants were a wondrous sign (Zech. 3:8). As priests, they represented and pointed to the coming Christ. The same can be said of the prophets. As lesser messiahs, Haggai, Zechariah, and Malachi contributed to God's revelation of the gospel simply by their status as prophets. In his messianic role, the prophet signaled and increased the anticipation for the coming Christ. Haggai, Zechariah, and Malachi were the last of God's installments on the prophetic line leading purposefully and unfailingly to the ideal Messiah. They shared the mission of John the Baptist, the greatest of the prophets before the ideal Prophet, to prepare the way for the coming of Christ. Being a little messiah was a big job. There is a sense in which every Christian is to be a sign of and to Christ just as the Old Testament prophets were. By our lives and words, we are to represent Christ and to point to Him. As Christians, we are "little christs." That is a big job too.

But our attention now is on the prophetic office and its significance for Haggai, Zechariah, and Malachi. Although these postexilic prophets were separated temporally from their preexilic counterparts, four common facts about the job of prophet put their and every prophetic ministry in perspective for us: their preparation, their practice, their purpose, and their problem.

Their Preparation

By simple definition, a prophet is God's representative before men, which is why the Lord Jesus is the ideal Prophet. The New Testament declared Christ to be the "brightness of his glory, and the express image of his person" (Heb. 1:3); and "the image of the invisible God" (Col. 1:15), in whom dwelt "all the fulness of the Godhead bodily" (Col. 2:9). The bottom line, then, is this: Jesus Christ is the ideal Prophet because He is God. Representing God is an awesome task, and the prophet's job description is prodigious. So consequential was the prophet's job that only a specially qualified person could dare take it on. Significantly, the essential qualifications had nothing to do with personal abilities; otherwise, none would ever have been prophets. Paul expressed a sentiment that applies to his Old Testament counterparts as well as to every minister of the gospel. Overwhelmed with the life-and-death issues of his ministry, he asked, "And who is sufficient for these things?" (2 Cor. 2:16), and then answered, "Our sufficiency is of God" (2 Cor. 3:5). How does one even begin preparing for such a weighty ministry?

Preparing for gospel ministry today follows a different paradigm than it did for the Old Testament prophets. Today, would-be ministers are expected to have a thorough seminary education covering all of the essential disciplines of theology. No such formal education for Old Testament prophets existed; a common misinterpretation suggests that the expression "sons of the prophets" refers to prophets-in-training. Rather, the expression simply designates those who belonged to the class of prophets. In other words, the "sons of the prophets" were prophets. But regardless of educational apprenticeship or lack thereof, two essential requisites for prophetic ministry were divine calling and divine equipping.

First, true prophets were *called* and *commissioned* by God. God did not open up the prophetic ministry to volunteers, and He dealt harshly with those who tried to usurp the position. False prophets, in fact, were under the sentence of death (Deut. 13:5; Jer. 28:15–17). But God chose those He wanted to represent Him, and His only criterion was His sovereign good pleasure. Being chosen for this special ministry was anything but a cause for pride. The divine principle is that God intentionally chooses foolish, weak, base, despised things and "things which are not, to bring to nought things that are" (1 Cor. 1:27–28). This is not to say that those with natural abilities or intellect were excluded from prophetic calling, but it does mean that God chose those whose personal gifts and abilities would not compete for His glory (1 Cor. 1:29).

Family was not an issue either. Apart from identifying Zechariah's father and grandfather (Ezra 5:1; Zech. 1:1) and placing him in the priestly line (Neh. 12:16), the Scripture says nothing more about his lineage and absolutely nothing about the lineage of either Haggai or Malachi. The lack of details about lineage is immaterial. Of the three anointed or messianic occupations, only the prophetic office was unrestricted regarding pedigree. Priests had to trace to Levi; kings (at least those of the southern kingdom) had to trace to Judah, and even more specifically to the family of David. So whereas priests and kings were born to be priests and kings, prophets became prophets only by the special call of God. Interestingly, whereas priests and kings could not cross over into the spheres of the others' operation, prophets could be priests, kings, or anything else. For the prophet, everything depended on God's call.

The Scripture does not record the initial divine calling of every prophet, but enough is revealed to establish the pattern. Jeremiah's call is a casebook example. The Lord's word to Jeremiah is particularly informative: "Before I formed you in the womb I knew you; before you were born I sanctified you; and I appointed you a prophet to the nations" (Jer. 1:5, author's translation). Three verbs express the nature of the divine choice. The Lord said that He *knew* Jeremiah. This is more than simple awareness or intellectual knowledge. It is, rather, an intimate, special, and selecting knowledge. This knowledge is part of the Old Testament's vocabulary of election. Humanly speaking, God knew Jeremiah before there was anything to know. The Lord then said that He *sanctified* him. Before Jeremiah was born, God had set him apart for the special purpose of being a prophet. His service was divinely determined before he knew what was happening. Finally, the Lord said that He *appointed* Jeremiah to be a prophet. Usually this verb has the meaning "to give," but it also has the special sense of appointing or assigning to a specific task. God chose Jeremiah to be a prophet; He called Jeremiah to be a prophet; and Jeremiah was a prophet. So it was for every other true prophet.

We may know nothing of the occasion or details of God's call to Haggai, Zechariah, and Malachi, but the fact of the call is evident from its consequence. That the Lord's word came to each (Hag. 1:1; Zech. 1:1; Mal. 1:1) is irrefutable verification that they were God's select spokesmen, His prophets. Just as God raised Jeremiah to speak for Him in the final hours before the captivity of the southern kingdom, so He raised these three to speak for Him to those who returned to the land after that captivity.

Second, prophets were divinely *equipped* and *enabled*. When the Lord anointed one for some sphere of service, He did not abandon that individual to his own abilities or ingenuity. The Lord always supplied the power for that service, with the ultimate agent of that power being the Holy Spirit. This empowering for service would have been the most vivid element in the anointing ceremony. As the olive oil was poured and smeared on the head of the appointed messiah, so the Holy Spirit came upon him to enable him to perform the ministry for which he was being consecrated.

Although there is no direct statement regarding the empowerment or inspiration by the Holy Spirit of these three, fulfilling the responsibilities of their office required it. What we read of this experience in the ministry of some prophets illustrates the common experience of all. Here,

Ezekiel is a casebook example. Immediately after his call to the prophetic office, Ezekiel witnessed a mysterious and magnificent vision of God's absolute glory and fell on his face in worship and recognition of self-insufficiency. The sight of the Lord incapacitated him. Then the Lord commanded him to stand, something that by himself he was incapable of doing. But then the Spirit entered him and caused him to stand, equipping and empowering him to do the very thing God commanded him to do (Ezek. 1:28–2:2). In another example, Micah testified, when contrasting his ministry with that of false prophets, that he was conscious of divine equipping: "But truly I am full of power by the spirit of the LORD, and of judgment, and of might, to declare unto Jacob his transgression, and to Israel his sin" (Mic. 3:8). Similarly, the Lord assured Isaiah in connection with a profound prophecy of the Redeemer coming to Zion: "My spirit that is upon thee, and my words which I have put in thy mouth, shall not depart out of thy mouth" (Isa. 59:21). So the Spirit's empowering prophets enabled them to fulfill their duty of obeying God's commands, to preach with boldness regardless of opposition, and to do so with the confidence of the ultimate success of the word they preached. That the writings of these prophets are included in the canon of sacred Scripture is irrefutable evidence of their being empowered by the Spirit: "For the prophecy came not in old time by the will of man: but holy men of God spake as they were moved by the Holy Ghost" (2 Peter 1:21). Poignantly, what Zechariah said to encourage Zerubbabel in his civic service applied equally to his own ministry: "Not by might, nor by power, but by my spirit,

saith the LORD of hosts" (Zech. 4:6). This divine energiz-
ing, enabling, and equipping overcame human weakness
and inabilities.

Their Practice

As representatives of God to men, prophets' principal func-
tion, not surprisingly, was to speak in God's behalf to men.
In a graphic sense, the prophet was the mouthpiece of God.
It is not without significance that Christ, the ideal Prophet,
owns as one of His titles "the Word" (John 1:1) and is the
One by whom God has spoken in these last days (Heb. 1:2).
As the ideal Prophet, Christ is God's final Word. Every
other true prophet spoke of Him.

The prophet's authority rested in the fact that he
was speaking the Lord's word to men. The Hebrew word
translated "prophet" implies something of the inherent authority in the prophet's words. It is formed from a
verb that most likely means simply "to speak." The word
"prophet" evidences the same pattern as the word "messiah" in that it conveys the passive idea of the verb. A
prophet, therefore, is one who has been spoken to and
who in turn conveys that divine message to men. The only
legitimate prophetic word—whether predicting the future,
exposing sin, or inviting repentance—was "thus saith the
Lord GOD" (Ezek. 2:4).

Comparing Exodus 4:10–16 with Exodus 7:1 provides
a clear illustration of the prophet's function. After receiving God's commission to deliver Israel from Egypt, Moses
expressed his reluctance, claiming his inability to speak
well. God then appointed Aaron to be the spokesman to

the people in behalf of Moses: "He shall be to thee instead of a mouth, and thou shalt be to him instead of God" (Ex. 4:16). In this spokesman capacity, Aaron is identified as a prophet (Ex. 7:1). He was to speak only what Moses had first spoken to him. Aaron's word equated to the word of Moses. So long as he spoke only what he was told to speak by Moses, all was well. When he ventured to speak on his own, there was trouble, as with the golden calf in Exodus 32. Thus it was for every prophet of the Lord. So long as he spoke the word of the Lord, he fulfilled his calling well. The prophet had no right just to give his own opinions on matters. When self-proclaimed prophets voiced their opinions, God forthrightly dismissed them; they had no authority (see Jer. 14:14). Although modern preachers do not share the same messianic office as the ancient inspired prophets, the principle of declaring only God's Word applies to them as well. The pulpit is no place for voicing or promulgating personal opinions; it is the place for declaring only what God has revealed in sacred Scripture.

Perhaps one of the clearest statements that the prophet was God's messenger with God's message is Haggai 1:12–13. Verse 12 actually equates obeying the voice of the Lord God with obeying the voice of Haggai the prophet. Verse 13 identifies Haggai as the "LORD's messenger" speaking "the LORD's message." Throughout each of the postexilic prophets is evidence that these were true prophets speaking only the word of the Lord. Statements such as "came the word of the LORD" (e.g., Hag. 1:3; Zech. 1:1, 7); "saith the LORD" (e.g., Hag. 1:7; Zech. 5:4; 8:2; Mal. 1:2; 3:7, 17); and "the burden of the word of the LORD" (Zech. 9:1; 12:1; Mal. 1:1) are scattered throughout the books.

In speaking in behalf of God as His mouthpiece, prophets were primarily preachers of that word. As preachers, they were concerned not only in imparting information to the intellect but also in stirring up the emotions and imploring willful responses to the word. They were reformers urging repentance, conformity, and obedience to God's covenant demands. The people were not only obliged to hear the word of the Lord but to heed it as well. Zechariah began his ministry by warning the people not to respond to his preaching like their ancestors did to the former pre-exilic prophets: "They did not hear, nor hearken unto me, saith the LORD" (Zech. 1:4).

Their Purpose

Although predictions of the future were not the principal part of their preaching, prophets incorporated them into their overall messages. Because the prophets were reformers, much of their message focused on God's past dealings with His people and His covenant stipulations. The postexilic prophets were no exception. For instance, Haggai argued on the basis of some of the old Levitical laws of cleanness and uncleanness (2:11–13). Zechariah referred to the preaching of the former prophets (1:4), used temple imagery (chap. 4), and exhorted obedience to God's moral law (8:16–17). Malachi reiterated the fact of God's patriarchal election (1:2–3), demanded priestly purity on the basis of God's covenant with Levi (2:4–5), and reasoned for family stability on the basis of God's creation (2:10). But like all the prophets before them, Haggai, Zechariah, and Malachi predicted the future as well.

This had to be the case since in the old dispensation predicting the future accurately was one way of distinguishing a false prophet from a true one. Through Moses, the Lord issued two tests to evaluate the legitimacy of a professed prophet. If a prophet preached contrary to truth that God had already revealed (for instance, serving another god), that would mark him as false (Deut. 13:1–4; 18:20). Paul put it this way: "And the spirits of the prophets are subject to the prophets" (1 Cor. 14:32). We should all imitate the practice of the Bereans, who "received the word with all readiness of mind, and searched the scriptures daily, whether those things were so" (Acts 17:11). Keeping Bibles open during preaching is a good practice, and biblical preachers never fear open Bibles.

The second test concerned the fulfillment of what the prophet said would happen (Deut. 18:22; Jer. 28:9). Predictions that did not pan out proved a prophet to be false. Consequently, predictions were part of prophetic preaching to authenticate the prophet. The Lord Jesus Himself, as the ideal Prophet, was subject to this test. The one prediction upon which Christ staked His entire prophetic credibility was the prophecy of His own resurrection (Matt. 12:40; John 2:19). The fact of the real, historic, bodily resurrection of Jesus was heaven's validation and verification of His entire prophetic office. If this most remarkable prediction was fulfilled, how much should man give heed to every other claim and statement Jesus made! That is the point, and all men should listen well. The point is the same for

Haggai, Zechariah, and Malachi. Their predictions validate their ministry and earn for them a hearing.

But their predictions were more than proofs of ministry; they were integral to their messages. Predictions were part of their motivational preaching, designed not to satisfy intellectual curiosity about the future but to affect contemporary life because of the certain future. These prophets were preaching to a people who had every reason to expect great blessing. In obedience they had returned to the Promised Land from what had become the comfort of captivity. Yet they were not experiencing the blessing they expected. Hostility from the outside and apathy from the inside seemed to stall the blessing. They were about to enter four hundred years of divine silence before the next prophetic voice; they needed a message to assure them that the end was not yet and better days were ahead. To that end, the predictions served four purposes.

First, prophecy *glorifies God by indicating that He is in control.* Because God rules, what will be is just as certain as what has been; His purpose will prevail. Prophecy is a dramatic way of displaying God's sovereignty, and thus it brings glory to Him. He knows the end from the beginning; therefore, He guarantees the end from the beginning. Nothing can frustrate or alter what He has determined. If God determines the future, it follows that He determines and controls the present as well, even with all its problems and things that are contrary to expectation. If nothing can frustrate His future purpose, nothing can frustrate His present purpose either.

Second, prophecy *encourages believers by inspiring confidence.* This confidence is the inevitable corollary to the assurance that God controls time and that regardless of appearances, the present is part of the execution of God's program. Looking in faith to the divinely revealed future should inspire confidence for service and duty by assuring the believer that his "now" fits precisely on the way to "then." A proper application of prophecy produces an active, bold, fervent, and confident performance of duty. So after Zechariah predicted God's promise of marvelous prosperity and peace (8:3–8), he admonished, "Let your hands be strong, ye that hear in these days these words by the mouth of the prophets" (8:9). Even though those particular people would not personally experience the full magnitude of that promise, they were to be zealous in doing what God had for them to do then. God's future must always affect our present.

Third, prophecy *intensifies the desire for God's will by increasing expectant hope.* Knowing what God has promised heightens the desire to experience and possess the promise. The more we contemplate the promise, the more we want the promise to materialize. The more details about the promise we know, the more intense the desire becomes. Prophecy is a means whereby God keeps hope alive and increases trust in and dependence on Him. Through prophecy, God incites us to want Him and what He has promised more than anything else.

Fourth, prophecy *motivates sinners to repentance and saints to purity by encouraging holiness.* If the Old Testament prophets teach anything about the use of prophecy, it is that prophecy motivates repentance and purity. Joel, for instance, after describing the great and terrible "day of the LORD" (2:11), issued a classic call to repentance: "Therefore also now, saith the LORD, turn ye even to me with all your heart, and with fasting, and with weeping, and with mourning: and rend your heart, and not your garments, and turn unto the LORD your God: for he is gracious and merciful, slow to anger, and of great kindness, and repenteth him of the evil" (2:12–13). The apostle Peter, describing the same Day of the Lord, concluded, "Seeing then that all these things shall be dissolved, what manner of persons ought ye to be in all holy conversation and godliness" (2 Peter 3:11). So Haggai implores his congregation to consider their ways (1:5, 7). Zechariah assures that if the people return or repent, then the Lord will return to them in blessing (1:3). Malachi describes the desirable blessing in store for those who truly fear the Lord (3:16–17; 4:3–4).

Their Problem

I say their problem, but the problem is really ours. The problem concerns how we should interpret prophecy, particularly the predictions. Every genre has its own peculiarities and principles of interpretation to safeguard the proper sense and to assure correct understanding. Interpreting poetry, for instance, is different from interpreting prose. If I told my wife that her hair looked like a flock of goats or that her neck looked like the tower of David, and she interpreted me literally, she would probably take it as an insult rather than a compliment, notwithstanding the biblical imagery (Song 4:1, 4). The point is poetry is different from prose, and so is prophecy. While growing up, I heard often that prophecy is simply prewritten history, as clear as yesterday's newspaper. I appreciate the God-honoring sentiment that generated that statement, but prophecy is not as clear as history. (Read the morning newspaper and then read Revelation, with its multiheaded and multihorned beasts, and form your own conclusion.) I maintain that every divinely inspired prophecy will be actually fulfilled; in that sense it is prewritten history. But clearly hindsight is a better interpreter than foresight. We must acknowledge, therefore, some important principles in anticipation of the prophetic language we are going to encounter in the postexilic prophets.

The nature of prophecy flows out of its fourfold purpose to glorify God, to encourage believers, to intensify desire for God's will, and to motivate sinners to repentance and saints to purity. Prophecy is designed to fuel faith, not to foster fatalism.

Prophetic Ambiguity

An intentional ambiguity inheres in prophecy. God reveals enough clarity to testify to His control of time and faithfulness to His word, but He does not make us privy to every detail of His plan. I often refer to 2 Kings 7 to illustrate this principle of prophecy because it contains two specific prophecies of Elisha and their literal fulfillments: cheap food and the destiny of the doubter. Samaria was under Syrian siege and was suffering great famine. Elisha's prediction of abundant and cheap food seemed impossible, and "a lord on whose hand the king leaned" let him know so.

That doubt precipitated the prediction that the lord would see it but not eat it (2 Kings 7:1–2). Both of these were very specific predictions. The details of the fulfillment, however, make it clear that Elisha left out some key facts. Had he delineated how the lepers would find the camp of the Syrians abandoned with all the cache of supplies, and how the doubter would be trampled by the hungry crowd rushing to buy some of the cheap food, the doubter would have been a fatalistic fool to accept the king's appointment to "have the charge of the gate" (2 Kings 7:17). But enough was revealed to make it absolutely certain that the whole episode was "according to the word of the LORD" (2 Kings 7:16). The prophecy was clear, yet ambiguous. Prophecy reveals much about the future, but it doesn't reveal everything. Remember that in Revelation 10, when John heard the seven thunders, God instructed the apostle not to write what was revealed to him. That prohibition to write tells us that we do not and cannot know everything about the future. We are to believe what God has revealed and trust Him for the rest. He lets us see enough to assure us that all time, including our times, are in His hand and under His control. We will have ample opportunity to see this in the postexilic prophets, especially in Zechariah.

Prophetic Language

Let me suggest some specific things to keep in mind about the nature of prophetic language. First, prophecy tends to use symbolic language that must be interpreted figuratively. This is particularly true in the special category of prophetic style called *apocalyptic prophecy.* Daniel is a casebook example of apocalyptic prophecy, and so are portions of Zechariah. For instance, Daniel's prediction of world empires in terms of strange, unnatural beasts cannot be interpreted literally without, quite frankly, being weird. Only science fiction would claim that a king of Greece was in reality a rough goat with a big horn between its eyes (Dan. 8:21). Let's not confuse an actual fulfillment of prophecy with a pedantically literal interpretation of prophetic language. The bestial symbolism of Daniel refers to actual empires. Some connection between the strange beasts and the kingdoms they represent has been and will be actually fulfilled. Interpreting symbolism requires that we determine the point of relevance between the symbol and the actual referent without attempting to find a tit-for-tat parallel. Zechariah's use of symbolism, from the colored talking horses to flying scrolls, will challenge our interpretive skills for sure. The meaning of symbolic language does not reside on the surface; discerning the meaning requires careful thought. That's fine: pondering Scripture always proves beneficial.

Second, prophecy tends to use the language of imminency. This means that regardless of how distant the prophecy from its actual fulfillment, the prediction is made as though its fulfillment were impending, about to occur. This intentional temporal ambiguity is one of the most significant features of prophetic language. Since the time of fulfillment is not specified, the application of the prophecy is not limited. For prophecies to be precisely dated would effectively rob a given prophecy of its purpose to affect the present of all the prefulfillment generations. So Malachi announced the sudden appearance of the Messenger of the covenant (Christ) into the temple even though that sudden appearance would not occur for four centuries (3:1). But the point was that they had best be ready.

There are other hermeneutical issues and concerns, but I think I have said enough for now about the nature of prophecy to prepare us for the specifics of Haggai, Zechariah, and Malachi. Biblical prophecy infallibly witnesses to God's absolute and sovereign control of time and circumstance. Some components of their prophecies have been fulfilled; some remain to be fulfilled. But truth is timelessly relevant. All the "then" truths of the past or of the future are "now" truths for us. It will be our principal concern as we make our way through these prophets not to chart out a sequence of events, as interesting as that may be, but to discover the truths for living from the pens of these men who served as the very mouthpiece of God in their generation and in ours. Their inspired sermons remain relevant. That is fact.

QUESTIONS

1. In what sense were prophets "messiahs"?

2. How does the "job" of every Christian parallel that of the prophets?

3. How does Christ qualify as the ideal Prophet?

4. Compare the qualifications of the three messianic functions or offices.

5. What can we learn about Jeremiah's call to ministry that applies to every prophet and, by extension, to every Christian?

6. In what sense can the prophets be understood as reformers?

7. What was the most important test of a true prophet, and why? How should that same test be used to evaluate every preacher?

8. How should biblical predictions affect you personally?

9. Why is it important that biblical predictions are not too specific regarding details?

2

Facts about Their Times

The Bible did not fall to earth from heaven complete and leather bound. The Old Testament alone was written over a period of about a thousand years by different men, all of whom were inspired by the Holy Spirit. But each one lived in his own time and place; each one reflected and addressed the specific issues of his day. The truths of the Bible are universally and timelessly relevant, but they were first given to a specific people at a specific time to meet specific needs. The ultimate objective of our study of the Bible is to understand those universal and timeless truths and to apply them to our specific times and needs. Therefore, an important part of Bible study is to learn what we can about the author, his times, and his particular circumstances. Haggai, Zechariah, and Malachi are postexilic prophets. *Postexilic* is a temporal designation that presupposes both exilic and preexilic periods as well. That these prophets are labeled chronologically suggests the importance of knowing something about the time.

Whereas many of the preexilic prophets dated their writings according to either the northern or southern kings during whose administrations they ministered, the exile marked the temporary end of kingship in Judah until Messiah would come (Ezek. 21:26–27). Consequently, Haggai and Zechariah, the first two of the postexilic prophets, both canonically and chronologically, dated their ministries according to the Persian King Darius (522–486 BC). Although Malachi does not make any explicit historical reference, reading between the lines dates his ministry about a hundred years later. I will address the specific dates of each book in due course, but my concern for now is simply to put them in the postexilic period, the latter part of the sixth century to just past the midway point of the fifth century BC, roughly the period from 520 to 435 BC for all three combined.

Assigning such specific dates to biblical books is a little complicated since our calendar reckoning differs from what was used in either Old Testament or New Testament times. But since our reckoning system is what we know and use, we customarily insert our own dates into the ancient time line. Plugging in our dates does not always yield precise results, but neither should it be regarded as mere guesswork. Scholars use two kinds of evidence for establishing these dates: relative chronologies and absolute chronologies. Relative chronologies involve simply putting names and events in sequential order. Absolute chronologies require the insertion of an actual calendar date in the sequence. These actual dates are often calculated from some ancient documentation mentioning an astronomical event, such as an eclipse. Although I am clueless as to how to calculate and deduce when and where eclipses occurred and will occur again, others, happily, are not. So we rely on those calculations and conclusions. The fortunate thing is that we have plenty of evidence from the ancient world, both from the Old Testament and from the people of Old Testament times, to establish fairly accurate chronologies. I'm not going to go into all the evidence for assigning these dates to Haggai, Zechariah, and Malachi, but I do want to emphasize that the dates are not just being pulled arbitrarily from some hat.

Dating the books is one thing; understanding the significance of the date is another. Factoring in what we know about Hebrew history with the overall history of the ancient Near East marks the sixth to fifth centuries BC as a climacteric point on the time line of world history. But to grasp the significance of the postexilic period, we need to back up and put it within the framework of the preexilic and exilic periods. Looking at this checkered history theologically and politically will provide insight into the message for their time.

The Theology of Their Time

These periods resonate with theological principles and reveal that God keeps His word—whether it is a word of promise or of threat. Comprehending the import of these three periods requires going back to the book of Deuteronomy. One of the great themes in Deuteronomy concerns God's promise of the land. God first promised the land as an integral element in the covenant He made with Abraham and his seed (Gen. 12:7; 15:18; 17:8). That promise was unilateral and unconditional. Although the promise concerned a real geographical territory whose borders can be found on a map, God infused the land promise with important spiritual and theological lessons. There was more to the land than dirt. Simplistically stated, throughout the Old Testament God used the land as an object lesson to represent the fullness of the spiritual blessing. Rest in the land was associated with the experience and enjoyment of God's presence. So notwithstanding the ultimately unconditional aspect of the promise, individual participation in the promise was conditioned by faith. Thus, according to Hebrews 3:19, the wilderness generation did not enter the land "because of unbelief" (see also the argument of Ps. 95:8–11). This is where the theology of Deuteronomy applies. Not only did entrance into the land require faith, so also did remaining in the land. Moses expressed clearly the terms of the land contract. First, if the people kept the commandments and walked in the ways of the Lord, the Lord would bless them richly in the land (see 28:1–2, 8–13). Second, if they violated the commandments, particularly by going after other gods, the Lord would curse them (28:14–15), primarily by plucking them out of the land and scattering them among the nations (28:63–64). Third, if they returned to the Lord, He would exercise compassion and graciously gather them from wherever they were scattered and bring them back to the land (30:2–3). That is a synopsis of preexile, exile, and postexile.

The checkered history of Israel mirrors each of these contractual points, and there is little hope of understanding any Old Testament prophet—preexilic, exilic, or postexilic—without factoring in the theology of Deuteronomy. Although Israel's faith was not unwavering nor their obedience perfect, several high-water marks in their spiritual development brought them victoriously into the land and enabled them to enjoy the promised prosperity and blessing. Sadly, it was not long before they tragically disobeyed and faithlessly pursued other gods. In keeping with His word, God expelled the people from the land, first the northern kingdom of Israel and then the southern kingdom of Judah. In one way or another all the prophets echoed Moses and warned the nation of the impending judgment; every preexilic prophet warned of potential exile. Perhaps more than any other preexilic prophet, Jeremiah picked up on the third point of Deuteronomy's theology and countered his message of imminent exile with hope of restoration after seventy years. The exile cured the people of many specific sins that caused the captivity, but it did not eradicate the problem of sin. Other issues arose that God addressed with a new slate of prophets. Impending exile was no longer the threat, but there were matters that required prophetic attention lest the progress of God's redemptive purpose leading to Christ be hindered. Here come Haggai, Zechariah, and Malachi.

The Politics of Their Time

While the Old Testament reveals the theological reasons for Israel's situations, the political history of the ancient Near East details the method by which God accomplished His purpose. Even a cursory survey of that history boldfaces the Lord's absolute sovereignty over all the affairs of the world to accomplish His purpose. Although the then-current events had military and political explanations that would have engaged the news media of the day, they evidence over and again the truth of Proverbs 21:1—"The king's heart is in the hand of the LORD, as the rivers of water: he turneth it whithersoever he will."

Because God is totally sovereign, He can choose to work either with or without external means to accomplish His will. The Lord's behind-the-scenes movement of nations was His primary method of executing the consequences stipulated in Israel's land contract. This means of accomplishing His will showed itself most obviously when the time came first for Israel and then for Judah to be expelled from the land because of their unbelief. The prophets Hosea and Amos, particularly, warned the northern kingdom that their rampant idolatry disqualified them from the land and that judgment loomed. Hearing the threat, however, did not cause them to pack their bags and leave their homes on their own. The Lord used the Assyrians as His instrument to effect the expulsion. Isaiah, with prophetic insight, identified the Assyrians as the rod of God's anger sent against the hypocritical nation (Isa. 10:5–6). From a natural historic perspective, it is not surprising that the Assyrians were able to conquer Israel. By the eighth century BC, Assyria had become the most powerful nation in the world of the Near East both militarily and politically, with its control extending throughout Mesopotamia all the way to Egypt. It ruled an empire. Secular accounts from the period detail a military genius and cruelty that stood unmatched. Certainly, neither Israel nor Judah possessed military machinery sufficient to resist Assyrian advance. But what is striking is the Assyrian policy of deportation used to control its conquered lands and people. Deportation was an ingenious way both to demoralize a people and to reduce the threat of rebellion. An expatriated people would have little incentive to revolt in a land that was not their native soil. Even more notable is that in the history of warfare, this seems to be the first time such a tactic was employed. In 722 BC, Samaria, the capital of Israel, fell to the Assyrians. Deuteronomy's threatened exile had begun. In the providence of God, at the very moment when His patience with idolatrous Israel had expired and the time of its expulsion had arrived, there was a mechanism in place to accomplish His word. Where did the Assyrian commanders get the idea of deportation? Remember from Proverbs 21:1 who holds and turns the king's heart.

It is equally remarkable that Judah did not fall to the Assyrians. Because the sin of the south was not yet ripe for judgment, Judah was preserved. God's direct intervention in protecting and preserving Judah showed that He was the one in control. During the administration of Hezekiah, God, without using any human means, caused the mighty army of Sennacherib to retreat in confusion after 185,000 of its soldiers were slain in the darkness of a single night (Isa. 37:36). But sadly, Judah's sin did ripen. Judah could not remain exempt from judgment. Virtually every prophet in the Old Testament warned the people that it was going to come. In the meantime the world went on, seemingly as normal. Not long before Judah's judgment, God dealt with the Assyrians. Nineveh, the capital city, fell to the combined armies of the Babylonians and Medes in 612 BC. Politics and power skirmishes followed, and Babylon ended up on top. In 605 BC, the Neo-Babylonian Empire began with Nebuchadnezzar at the head. He continued the Assyrian policy of deportation, and Judah's exile ensued. It worked for the Assyrians; it would work as well for the Babylonians. The first wave occurred in 605 BC. Daniel was a part of this wave. The second occurred in 597 BC. King Jehoiachin, Ezekiel, and ten thousand others were part of this one. The third occurred in 586 BC. This was the big one in which Jerusalem and the temple were destroyed. On the surface what happened during this period was just the stuff of world events: Babylon was on a roll. Above the surface what happened was the direct operation of God's will on earth. God was on the throne.

One final observation remains. The third element in Deuteronomy's land contract concerned the return to the land. Jeremiah, who declared that the loss of land was God's will, also announced God's will to restore the land in seventy years. The execution of this return was just as much in God's hand and control as the exile. For seventy years the world went on. Babylonian king followed Babylonian king until finally, in the normal course of human events, one regime replaced another. In 539 or 538 BC, a coalition between the Medes (the former allies of Babylon) and Persians under the command of Cyrus defeated the Babylonians. This is the same Cyrus that Isaiah had named a couple of hundred years earlier, identifying him as God's shepherd and God's anointed who would perform all of God's pleasure by ordering the rebuilding of Jerusalem (Isa. 44:28–45:1). At the beginning of his administration, Cyrus issued a decree that the peoples who had been exiled during the Assyrian and Babylonian Empires, who were now scattered throughout his even larger kingdom, could return to their homelands. Cyrus even subsidized the rebuilding projects, a wise strategy to ensure stability and peaceful loyalty throughout the vast Medo-Persian Empire. The exiles of Judah were included. At the precise moment when in the purpose of God it was time for Judah to return to the land, a mechanism was in place to effect that purpose. Where did Cyrus get the idea to let the exiles return? Remember Proverbs 21:1 and the One who holds and turns the king's heart.

Just as Judah's exile occurred in three stages (605, 597, and 586 BC), so did its return to the land after the exile. The first wave was in 536 BC in response to the edict of Cyrus. This group, under the leadership of Zerubbabel, was commissioned with the first order of business to build the temple that had been razed by the Babylonians. Ezra 1–6 records the history of this period. It was in connection with this first wave that Haggai and Zechariah prophesied. Notably, the historical circumstances recorded in Esther take place in Persia after the events of Ezra 6 but before Ezra 7. Consequently, the canonical order does not quite correspond to the historical sequence of events. Zechariah's ministry extended into Esther's time as well. The second wave occurred in 458 BC. Ezra was the principal character and was commissioned with the responsibility of building up the people spiritually. Ezra 7–10 records the history of this period. The third wave under the leadership of Nehemiah occurred in 445 BC. His responsibility was to build the walls of Jerusalem. The book of Nehemiah records the history of this period. Malachi would have been a contemporary with Nehemiah. Significantly, at each stage, the

Persian administration acted in some way to foster the success of the work of restoration.

Although Cyrus and the Assyrian and Babylonian kings before him were ignorant of God's movement of them and their role as the agents of divine providence, they were nonetheless subjects of God's kingdom. God certainly held them accountable for their transgressions against His law and dealt with them according to their works, but not even the worst of them could jeopardize God's agenda. The heart of every one of those kings was in God's hand, and He turned it in whatever way He desired to accomplish His will. In hindsight, it does not require much spiritual acumen to recognize God's amazing control over the nations of the Old Testament world. So at what point in the history of the world did God stop controlling the nations of the world?

In our hearts we know the biblically correct answer to this question. In our heart of hearts we know that God controls governments and the course of human events as much today as ever. Yet so often we live as though God at some point in history abdicated His throne in exchange for a bleacher seat. Too many Christians live as though God is pacing back and forth in heaven wondering what He will or can do if this or that political party gains power. At the very least, that is not a biblical view of God. Everything is still under His control.

There is far too much Persian history to consider here, but I think we have surveyed enough to get to the point. Old Testament history runs out before the end of the Persian Empire. The postexilic books, both prophetic (Haggai and Zechariah) and historic (Chronicles, Ezra, Nehemiah, and Esther), mention by name the Persian kings whose administrations had direct bearing on the progress of redemptive history: Cyrus, Darius I, Xerxes (Ahasuerus), and Artaxerxes I. God raised them up and used them well for His own glorious purpose.

The following chart of key events and characters leading to the ministries of Haggai, Zechariah, and Malachi may help you keep things straight as you sort through the history of the period. A lot was going on, and God used every bit of it to achieve His purpose and plan.

Judah	Babylon	Media-Persia
Josiah (640–609)* killed at Megiddo by Necho II	Neo-Babylonian Empire established (626) Nabopolassar (626–605) Alliance with Medes to destroy Nineveh (612)	
Jehoahaz (609) captured by Egyptians		
Jehoiakim (609–598) Daniel's exile (605)	Battle of Carchemish (605) Nebuchadnezzar (605–562)	
Jehoiachin (598–597) Deportation to Babylon (597)		

Judah	Babylon	Media-Persia
Zedekiah (597–587) Fall of Jerusalem and deportation to Babylon (587/586)		
Babylonian exile (587–538)	Amel-Marduk (562–560) Neriglissar (560–556) Labashi-Marduk (556) Nabonidus (556–539) (Belshazzar as coregent)	Astyages, king of Media (585–550) Cyrus's conquest of Media/beginning of Persian Empire (550)
Edict of Cyrus (538)	Fall of Babylon (539)	Cyrus (550–530)
Sheshbazzar's return (538) Zerubbabel's return (536) **Haggai and Zechariah**		Cambyses (530–522) Darius I (522–486)
Temple finished (516) Time of Esther (479–473) Ezra's return (458) Nehemiah (445–433) **Malachi**		Xerxes (486–465) Artaxerxes I (465–424) Darius II (423–404)

*All dates BC

The Message for Their Time

God's word is always in season, appropriate, and relevant. The messages God gave through Haggai, Zechariah, and Malachi were precisely what the people then needed to hear. The seventy-year exile marked the lowest point in the history of the covenant nation. The decree of Cyrus allowing and encouraging the expatriates to return to the homeland heralded the dawn of a new day. The prospect of peace, prosperity, and even the long-promised Messiah seemed to be immediately at hand. This was going to be the eve of all the utopian promises of the former prophets. The buzz of blessing was in the air.

A remnant returned in hope that God would keep His promise of restoration. The fullness of time was steadily approaching, and many things had to be in place for the coming Messiah. This generation had a crucial part to play in the drama of God's unfailing plan of redemption. A people, a city, and a temple had to be in place in the Promised Land in preparation for the coming Christ. But the serpent and its seed were still active and still hostile and full of enmity against the promised Seed of the woman, the Christ (Gen. 3:15). It was not long before those who returned to Judah with such high hopes faced opposition from the Samaritans, discouragement from the overwhelming desolation of the land, and dismay over the enormous size of the tasks. Hope faded away, and progress toward restoring the temple ceased. But a standing temple was integral to the Messiah's work; this was a critical moment.

God always has a word for His people at critical times. At the very time the work on the temple ceased in the second year of Darius (Ezra 4:24), God sent the prophets Haggai and Zechariah to address the problem (Ezra 5:1). Haggai and Zechariah preached to the same people about the same problem, but from different angles. Haggai did not mince words and employed a bit of guilt preaching as motivation. His purpose was to inspire the people to renewed dedication and determination for the work of the kingdom, to convince them that nothing was more important than kingdom work. He exhorted the people to reevaluate their priorities, making sure to put God first. Zechariah, on the other hand, used hope in the divinely guaranteed future as motivation. His purpose was to encourage God's people to live in victory and serve with diligence in view of the certain blessing God had purposed and promised. He encouraged the people to hope in the certainty of God's word.

But Haggai's guilt preaching was not designed to beat the people up or to leave them wallowing in self-despair. It was a means of getting the people to look away from themselves to the Messiah. He did this both directly and indirectly through typology or picture prophecies. Zechariah's promise preaching was not designed to create a cross-your-fingers kind of hope that was nothing more than wishful thinking. Rather, it pointed the people to the Messiah principally by those symbolic visions and direct predictions. We will consider specific texts in the analysis of each book. My point for now is that by preaching Christ, Haggai and Zechariah successfully motivated the people to do what they needed to do. They began preaching in 520 BC, and by 516 BC the temple was completed. Both prophets serve as reminders that Christ is the answer to every problem. That is as true today as it was then, so as we work our way through these prophets we must keep our eyes open for Christ.

The problem was a bit different for Malachi, but the answer was much the same. By proclaiming the blessing and glory associated with the coming Messiah, Haggai and Zechariah had moved their generation to rebuild the temple in preparation. But now almost one hundred years had passed, and there was no sign of the anticipated blessing. The nation was still under foreign domination, and there was no prospect in sight for a new king to sit on David's throne. Because they were not experiencing the promised blessings in the way they thought they should be, they grew impatient with God and doubted His ability to keep His word. Those misconceptions affected their view and practice of worship. Malachi's purpose was to awaken a people whose religious cynicism and skepticism of God's promises led to careless and dead worship and to renew hope and revive true religion in view of the certainty of God's purpose. He exposed and rebuked the insincerity of their religion, making it clear that the lack of blessing was not due to God's unfaithfulness or inability, but to their spiritual deadness.

With irrefutable evidence and logic, Malachi exposed the sin issues of a people who were decaying in dead religion. In so doing, he preached the gospel: death for sinners and life for saints. A day of judgment was coming that would turn the wicked to stubble (4:1), and a day of deliverance was coming for the righteous, who would experience life through the Sun of Righteousness (4:2). This life-giving

Sun is also identified as the Messenger of the covenant who would purify the people (3:1–3), both of which are messianic titles. Malachi preached a Christ who would come in God's perfect timing. Seeing Christ infuses life into religion. That was the answer to dead and formal worship in Malachi's day; it is the same answer for heartless worship today.

Over two-and-one-half millennia separate us from the postexilic prophets. Admittedly, that is a long time. Yet the issues faced by Israel then are not vastly different from those faced by the church today. Characters go by other names and surface details differ, but there is a commonality that makes for easy and necessary transfer of the "then" messages to now. So as we begin our survey of the messages of these last prophets before the Christian era, let us regard them not as ancient voices but as visiting preachers to our modern pulpits.

QUESTIONS

1. What is the difference between relative and absolute chronologies?

2. Why is Deuteronomy so important for understanding Old Testament prophets?

3. Explain how Proverbs 21:1 sums up ancient Near Eastern history.

4. How and why do many Christians act like Proverbs 21:1 does not apply to current events?

5. Make note of the three pivotal dates for Judah's exile and the three pivotal dates marking the end of the exile.

6. Contrast the approaches of Haggai and Zechariah to the same issues or needs in the nation.

7. What do all three postexilic prophets share in common as the ultimate answer to the problems of the nation?

8. How does that answer apply to issues of life and the church today?

Oct. D. Lauten - Chpt. 3-5

True joy comes from serving the Lord

1- facts about Haggai
2- Skewed views of priorities
3- Skewed " " service

1- Haggai is God's spokesperson - direct out of love to rebuild temple. People of God have lost God's vision for them; spiritual amnesia God's rebuilding temple, their lives. He's given us talents; renewed dedication

PART 2

Haggai: The Realist

2- H. rebukes people for putting themselves first. The Jews didn't want to work, it was difficult. Opposition were in a battle.
This world does not satisfy. What do we delight in? Christians seek to please our Lord.

Temple was for sacrifice to please a Holy God. O.T. temple - sign that pts to covenant relationship w/ God. Jews made themselves homes but let temple remained in ruins.

They obeyed the voice of God thru Haggai. One sermon turned them around.
They feared the Lord v. 12
They became doers of the Word.

$\longrightarrow$

Chpt. 5

Now what I'm doing ties into what
God is doing.

appearance - temple would not be
as grand - reality.

what I'm doing fall's short of what
happened in past.

BIG CHURCH doesn't mean success.
It's faithfullness. God looks
at heart! Live by faith in
ministry. v.9

GLORY of Jesus - fulfillment of
Jesus - greater glory

God is at work + bring glory
to Jesus.

3

Facts about Haggai

Haggai's job was the same as every other true prophet; he was God's representative and spokesman. It is said specifically of Haggai, however, that he was "the LORD's messenger in the LORD's message unto the people" (1:13). Consequently, obeying "the words of Haggai the prophet" equates to obeying "the voice of the LORD" (1:12). A frequent repetition in this short prophecy is that God spoke, and that His word came directly to Haggai. The divine source of the message is repeated so frequently that it is conspicuous even with a cursory reading. Robert Bell has charted out the data that highlight this important idea, identifying the different expressions that make the point. He notes that there are twenty-six references to God's word: "A conservative count of the Hebrew words used in these various phrases indicates that 17% of the book (102 of 600 words) focuses on the theme of God's word."[1] That is remarkable authority, and it demanded the attention of Haggai's congregation. It demands our attention because it is the word of the ever-living and never-changing God.

The facts covered in part 1 apply to Haggai and should be factored into our understanding of his ministry and circumstances. However, there are some specific introductory facts unique to Haggai to consider before we learn the lessons of his message.

The Man

In the Old Testament, names are often significant, having some connection to a person's character or behavior. This is particularly the case when the narrative explains the reasoning behind the name, such as Jacob (Gen. 25:26), or on the occasion of a name change, such as Jacob to Israel (Gen. 32:27–28). This is certainly the case regarding divine names that declare some propositional truth about the Lord. There are even times when we can create a link between a prophet's name and his message. Zechariah means "Jehovah remembers," and it is not hard to connect that meaning to Zechariah's emphasis of God's keeping His promise. But other times, more often than not, individual names were just labels of identification, much the way we tend to think of names. My name is Michael, and it has significant meaning in Hebrew, posing the question, Who is like God? But my parents did not know Hebrew and were not making a theological point in naming me. They evidently liked the name or, at best, thought of the angelic name at the sight of my then angelic appearance. The point is that, notwithstanding the translation of my name, the meaning is irrelevant to getting my attention. Haggai's name means "festal one." Haggai was his name, but there was nothing festive about his message. He assured the people of a glorious future, but not before rebuking them sternly and warning them of the consequences of disobedience.

This is why, in part, I refer to Haggai as the realist. Remember, he was commissioned to address the delay in building the temple. For certain, external opposition from those hostile to God's purpose was the initial hindrance in causing the delay (see Ezra 4), but Haggai cuts right to the chase, identifying the real problem to be with the people who had lost their vision for the work of God. Their priorities were skewed, and Haggai let them know it without mincing any words.

Perhaps his age also contributed to his realism. Maturity tends to puts things in perspective. I started to describe his age as "old," but even that is a matter of perspective. I used to think my age was old, but now I know better. My guess is if I ever reach Haggai's probable age, the notion of old will still be ahead. But in all likelihood, Haggai was the elder alongside Zechariah. Many interpreters regard his question in 2:3, "Who is left among you that saw this house in her first glory?" as an indication that Haggai himself was part of that group. Since the temple was destroyed in 586 BC, the captivity lasted for seventy years, and this prophecy dates to 520 BC, Haggai would have been in his midseventies when the foundation of the second temple was laid, and even a bit older when he preached the messages recorded in this prophecy. His prophetic ministry could have begun earlier, but this was his inspired recorded preaching. Along with Obadiah and Nahum, Haggai is one of the shortest of all the Shorter (Minor) Prophets. He got right to the point. Not uniquely or universally so, but that is a mark of maturity.

The Method and Message

Haggai framed his short and sometimes not-so-sweet message within chronological references, similar to Ezekiel's thirteen chronological statements that defined the structure of his argument (Ezek. 1:1; 8:1; 20:1; 24:1; 26:1; 29:1, 17; 30:20; 31:1; 32:1, 17; 33:21; 40:1). In fact, six dates mark the linear development of Haggai's recorded ministry: 1:1, 15; 2:1, 10, 18, 20. These dates range from the sixth to the ninth months, corresponding roughly to the four-month period of September to December according to our calendar.

Virtually every outline of Haggai that I've ever seen structures the book according to these chronological references. That is good because it is obvious and intended. There is some disagreement, however, as to whether each of the dates bears the same structural weight. I suggest that four of the date references are structural markers (1:1; 2:1, 10, 20), and two are incidental (1:15; 2:18). The four structural markers share the statement that the Lord's word came to Haggai on that particular day. The last two dated messages occur on the same day, so the text specifically says that the word of the Lord came again the second time to Haggai on that date. The focus obviously is more on the source of the message than when the messenger delivered it. Remember that Haggai was the Lord's messenger in the Lord's message. The dates function as literary devices to signal progression of argument rather than as simple marks on a calendar to trace chronology.

The first incidental date (1:15) marks the positive response of Zerubbabel, Joshua, and the people to Haggai's initial rebuke concerning the skewed priorities that contributed to their neglect of temple reconstruction. In just over three weeks after his first sermon, the entire remnant "came and did work in the house of the LORD of hosts, their God" (1:14). God raised Haggai to motivate the people to get back to building the temple, and that is what they did. The brevity of Haggai's ministry may trace to the response of the people. In essence, he preached himself out of a job. He had a couple more messages to encourage them to stay on track, but his job was done. The second incidental date (2:18) was to be the red-letter day from which the people were to mark the beginning of God's blessing. Although the temple was not yet completed and the harvest was not yet gathered, the Lord assured them that "from this day will I bless you" (2:19). That indeed was a date to mark on the calendar.

So on the basis of Haggai's method of dating his messages, it is possible to construct an outline of his four-month sermon series. He delivered the first message on 6/1/520 BC. In this first message (1:1–11), he rebukes the people for their skewed priorities of putting their own concerns and comforts before the work of the Lord. This is immediately followed by a short narrative of the people's positive response of obeying the "voice of the LORD" and "the words of Haggai" (1:12–15). But since the narrative of response does not constitute a separate sermon, for the sake of the outline I include it under point 1.

Haggai delivered the second message on 7/21/520 BC. In this second message (2:1–9), he reassures the people that they are doing the right thing by working on the temple even though appearances seem contrary to their expectations. He reassures them of God's presence and His purpose to fill this house with greater glory than the first temple. That greater glory will come with the Messiah, who will appear suddenly into this second temple (see Mal. 3:1). More on that later, but this second address is a christological high-water mark in Haggai's preaching.

The third message occurred on 9/24/520 BC. In this third message (2:10–19), Haggai encourages the people to continued obedience by reminding them of the contrasting consequences of disobedience and obedience. They were to remember the tragedies of the past and to count on the prospects for the future.

He preached his last recorded message on the same day, 9/24/520 BC. In this fourth message (2:20–23), Haggai sounds a bit more like his younger colleague, Zechariah, than his normally directly to-the-point self with his use of apocalyptic-sounding language and typological symbolism. But notwithstanding the shift in style, the point is clear as he assures the people of a certain future in which all the kingdoms of the world will fail, and God's kingdom and Messiah will prevail. It is a great last sermon.

An outline, then, looks like this:

I. Rebuke and Response Regarding the Temple Work (1:1–15)
II. Reassurances Regarding the Temple Work (2:1–9)
III. Incentives for Obedience (2:10–19)
IV. Assurances Regarding a Certain Future (2:20–23)

Although each section has a particular point of emphasis, Haggai weaves common themes throughout. Bell identifies the principal recurring themes as revelation, punishment, worship, blessing, and fellowship.[2] But the overarching theme is clearly on the surface throughout: to rebuild the temple by putting God first. Nothing is more important than kingdom work. Putting self first or feeling sorry for self is always going to be deleterious to the work of the Lord. Haggai sought to convince the people of that by inspiring them to renewed dedication and determination to making God's cause preeminent.

The particular matter of temple reconstruction that Haggai addressed has been resolved and replaced by a long succession of other issues that have suffered from the same kind of selfish attitude. Every generation and every individual must wrestle with the concern about priorities. Selfishness and self-pity are natural; making God and the work of the kingdom the supreme priority in life is not natural. But it is the proper perspective that every Christian should have. It takes grace, but that is not a problem. So even though Haggai dated his messages, his messages are not outdated.

QUESTIONS

1. Explain why Haggai is fittingly called the realist.

2. What was the principal problem among the people that Haggai addressed?

3. What evidence is there that Haggai was an old man at the time of his writing?

4. What structural clue suggests how best to outline Haggai's messages?

5. Why was Haggai's ministry so short-lived?

6. What makes Haggai's last message distinct from his others?

7. Why is it so easy for self-concerns to take precedence over spiritual or kingdom issues?

It's Not about You

Cyrus issued the decree that allowed the Jews to come back home to rebuild the temple, both subsidizing the project (Ezra 1:4) and restoring the temple utensils that Nebuchadnezzar had taken as booty when he ransacked and razed Jerusalem years earlier (Ezra 1:7). Surprisingly, not everybody jumped at the chance to return. But a remnant of repatriates responded, including some of the heads of Judah and Benjamin and the priests and Levites, "with all them whose spirit God had raised, to go up to build the house of the LORD which is in Jerusalem" (Ezra 1:5). They returned bent on their mission, first under the leadership of Sheshbazzar, whom Cyrus had appointed as governor (Ezra 5:14). Although he is designated as "the prince of Judah" (Ezra 1:8), this does not mean that he was a son of royalty, a king-in-waiting. The word translated "prince" means literally "one who has been raised up"; Sheshbazzar was an exalted leader, one elevated to be a civil authority. Under his leadership, work on the temple's foundation commenced (Ezra 5:16). It was a good start—but it was only the start.

It seemed that those who returned were so eager to reinstate the rituals and routines of worship that they

couldn't wait for the foundation to be laid before erect-
ing an altar for burnt offerings and keeping the Feast of
Tabernacles. This feast significantly commemorated the
wilderness wanderings and testified to the people's conscious sense of dependence on God for every provision of
life (Ezra 3:1–6). This was a lesson, unfortunately, that they
would soon forget. According to Ezra's narrative (3:2), this
initial progress was under the direction of Joshua, the high
priest of Aaron's line, and Zerubbabel, of the royal line of
David through Jeconiah (1 Chron. 3:17–19), both of whom
became principal characters in the combined preaching of
Haggai and Zechariah.

The exact relationship between Zerubbabel and Sheshbazzar is a matter of dispute. Although some suggest they
are the same person, the consensus is that they are indeed
different individuals. Unquestionably, Cyrus appointed
Sheshbazzar as the superintendent or governor over the
repatriates (Ezra 1:8; 5:14). Unquestionably, Zerubbabel
became prominent (perhaps due to his royal lineage) in the
homecoming events, and at least by the time of Haggai and
Zechariah had replaced Sheshbazzar as the civil authority.
Zechariah credits him with laying the foundation (finishing
what Sheshbazzar started) and ultimately with completing
the whole temple (Zech. 4:9). All this may seem beside the
point, but it is significant because it underscores Zerubbabel's connection to David's royal seed. Zerubbabel plays an
active role in rebuilding the temple in keeping with God's
covenant word to David that his seed would build the house
of the Lord. Solomon built the first one; Zerubbabel built
the second. He was not a king, but he qualified as David's

seed. It has bearing as well on Haggai's use of Zerubbabel as a messianic type (Hag. 2:20–23), which I will discuss later.

But all this information that may seem to be beside the point sets up the point of Haggai's first message. The initial enthusiasm and energy displayed at the beginning soon dissipated in the face of opposition. Adversaries "weakened the hands of the people of Judah, and troubled them in building, and hired counsellors against them, to frustrate their purpose, all the days of Cyrus king of Persia, even until the reign of Darius king of Persia" (Ezra 4:4–5). Given that Cyrus issued his edict in 538 BC, that it took some time to lay the foundation, that Darius began to rule in 522 BC, and that Haggai and Zechariah began to preach in the second year of Darius (520 BC), a conservative estimate would indicate that no work was done on the temple for ten to fifteen years.

During those ten to fifteen years, the stuff of life took over, and the work on the temple took last place on the list of priorities. Haggai's first message addresses the issue of the skewed priorities head-on. He makes it unmistakably clear that nothing is more important than kingdom work, and God's cause is to have preeminence over every other issue and concern of life. Or, to put it directly, Haggai told the people, "It's not about you." His first message is a stern rebuke (1:1–11), which happily was followed by a positive response from the leadership specifically and the people at large (1:12–15).

The Rebuke

Even the timing of Haggai's first sermon punctuated the problem he was going to address. He received and delivered

his first message on the first day of the month (1:1). According to the Levitical liturgy, the first of the month was a day
of special sacrifices and trumpet music designed to be a distinctive memorial before the Lord (Num. 10:10; 28:11–15).
But without the temple, the place where the sacrifices were
to be offered, the celebration was impossible. So on a day
when the temple was especially needed, Haggai rebuked
the people for the temple's not being there. The people had
to reevaluate their priorities. Twice in this short sermon,
Haggai instructed them, "Consider your ways" (1:5, 7). The
Hebrew says literally, "Set your heart upon your ways." In
the Old Testament, the "heart" refers to the entire inner
man, including the mind, emotions, and will. The word
"ways" refers to the customs and habits of life. Haggai was
calling for a change in thinking, feeling, and doing. The
problem was serious, and the solution had to be pervasive.

The work on the temple ceased because of circumstances and opposition beyond the people's control, but
the forced delay soon caused them to lose their vision and
sense of mission. It is natural for zeal to abate when out-
comes and circumstances are contrary to expectations.
Haggai put his finger on two core issues that are far too
common among God's people when things don't happen
according to plan, or at least according to their perception
of the plan.

Reinterpretation of God's Word

The tension between creed (what is believed) and circumstance (what is experienced) is very much a part of the
life of faith. God's people are to walk by faith, not by sight

(2 Cor. 5:7), but the physical eye often overrides the heart. Spiritually, appearance and reality are seldom the same, but what is seen tends to blur what is actually the fact. That puts faith at risk.

Failing to resolve this tension properly accounts for the people's excuse for not finishing the temple project: "The time is not come, the time that the LORD's house should be built" (1:2). They assumed that if God really intended for them to build the temple, there would have been no opposition. They had apparently equated doing God's will with tranquility, with smooth sailing. Initially, with enthusiasm and hyperenergy, they expended themselves in the construction work. But they had no sooner started than they had to stop because of outside opposition. They thought the only explanation was that it wasn't God's will for them to build the temple after all. If it really were the time, then everything would have fallen in place since no one and nothing can frustrate or alter God's will.

This conclusion was contrary to plenty of evidence. Jeremiah, moved by the Holy Spirit, had said it was time. The seventy years were up (Jer. 29:10–14). Cyrus, unconsciously moved by God, had said it was time. Isaiah, long before Cyrus was even born, had said that he would say to Jerusalem, "Thou shalt be built; and to the temple, Thy foundation shall be laid" (Isa. 44:28). Ezra records that he actually said it to these very people (Ezra 1:1–4; see also 2 Chron. 36:22–23). God's word was objectively and unmistakably clear: it was time to build the temple. But the Samaritans said no (Ezra 4:4–5). The people could not see God, but they saw the Samaritans plainly. So sight prevailed, and they reinterpreted God's word to mean it was not the time. It is a common and comfortable resolution when experience clashes with doctrine to redefine the doctrine. Whittling truth to shape it to experience makes it easier to believe.

This reinterpretation of God's word and will reveals some wrong thinking. First, they were not thinking rightly about God's power as it relates to His plan. God's plan is certain, and His power guarantees its success. That does not mean, however, that there will not be opposition and hostile efforts to thwart His plans and purposes. The fact is that God is so powerful and so much in control that He intentionally factors in opposition as part of His plan to highlight the greatness of His power over the greatest of the powers of evil. This principle is clear from the first revelation and declaration of God's redemptive plan in Genesis 3:15. God announced both the persistent hostility of the serpent's seed as well as the ultimate victory of the woman's Seed. That statement set the course of redemptive history and is illustrated repeatedly throughout Scripture. For instance, God assured Moses that He would bring the people out from Egyptian bondage (Ex. 3:12), and then He informed Moses that Pharaoh would oppose the exodus because He would "harden his heart, that he shall not let the people go" (Ex. 4:21). But Pharaoh's opposition was the opportunity for God to show His wonders and might so that deliverance would be to God's glory, and not evidence of Pharaoh's generosity (Ex. 3:19–20). So when the Samaritans raised their opposition to the work, the people should have interpreted the hostility as evidence of God's plan coming together. Faith in the certainty of God's word is the link between creed and circumstance. Rather than redefining the creed to make it conform to circumstance, faith interprets circumstance as the means God is using to accomplish His end. That means glory for Him and good for His people.

Second, they were not thinking rightly about the gospel—a serious miscalculation! The temple was more than just a place; it was a visible sermon of the gospel. It stood as a symbol or object lesson of God's presence with His people and of the sacrifices that were necessary for unholy man to have fellowship with the most holy God. Even more significantly, as a divinely defined object lesson, it was a type or picture-prophecy of God's incarnation, the climactic manifestation of God's presence in the coming of Jesus, who was Immanuel ("God with us"). The temple not only predicted Christ's coming but also pictured His once-and-final sacrifice by the repeated sacrifices of the temple routines. Neglecting work on the temple was tantamount to forgetting the gospel. Whenever God's people are not consciously factoring the gospel in the issues of life, there is going to be some serious backsliding, to say the least. Years later, Paul addressed the same point to the Corinthians when he asserted that self-interests must give way in light of what Christ has done (2 Cor. 5:14–15). Haggai's congregation should have been looking to the same Christ.

Redirection of Effort
The second point of Haggai's rebuke exposed the people's error of redirecting their efforts from God's work to self-interests. They thought that it was not time to rebuild the

temple, but it was time to remodel their own homes, most likely with cedar panels—perhaps with the very planks that had been stockpiled for temple reconstruction (1:4). The first temple had walls of cedar (1 Kings 6:15), so most likely cedar would have been used in the second as well. Confessedly, I'm only speculating here, but there must have been a lot of wood just sitting around not being used. But regardless of where the cedar planks came from, the point is that the people's priorities had shifted from kingdom work to personal concerns. Religion was now on the border of life.

As is so often the case when personal survival or advancement becomes the chief concern, satisfaction or contentment is elusive. Haggai describes the consequence of the people's misplaced priorities in images that are all too common. Life had become the proverbial rat race (1:6). Investments were not profitable (much sowing, but little harvest); the necessities of life (food, drink, and clothing) were never enough; they lived paycheck to paycheck (wages were put into bags with holes). Putting self first is ultimately always self-defeating and never satisfying. When things become more important than God, there can never be enough things to bring contentment.

This frustrating and futile lifestyle traces directly to the people's skewed priorities. The Lord made that pointedly clear: "Ye looked for much, and, lo, it came to little; and when ye brought it home, I did blow upon it. Why? saith the LORD of hosts. Because of mine house that is waste, and ye run every man unto his own house" (1:9). Ironically, even though they were back in the Promised Land, their backsliding regarding the temple work put them under curse conditions. The state of affairs Haggai describes (1:6, 10–11 particularly) sounds very much like the curses Moses predicted for disobedience and covenant unfaithfulness (Deut. 28:15–68). Not having God and kingdom work as the main priority of life is serious. Putting God first is an expression of the greatest commandment to love Him totally (Deut. 6:5). It is the sobering conclusion that if loving God totally is the greatest commandment, then not loving Him and not making Him the first priority is the greatest sin.

Yet there was hope if they redirected their efforts—this time away from self back to the Lord. If they would get back to the work of rebuilding the temple, God would be pleased and would be glorified (1:8). Repentance works. God gives His word on it (saith the Lord).

The Response

I've often thought that preachers and flight attendants have a lot in common. Prior to takeoff, flight attendants review and demonstrate various safety procedures designed to prevent injury and even to preserve life in cases of emergency. Notwithstanding how crucial the instructions, most passengers have no sense of urgency and rudely ignore the message by engaging in awkward conversations with next-seat strangers, by reading, by sleeping, or just by being bored and inattentive. Similarly, preachers—with a far greater lifesaving message—experience the same kind of inattention. The unhappy fact is that few sermons are remembered beyond the moment of delivery, and even fewer beyond the church parking lot. Most churchgoers expect a lot from preachers—to give diligence to the pulpit ministry, to hold their attention—but only a few seem to get anything from them. Sadly, this kind of response to preaching has a long history. The Lord Himself said to the generation on the eve of destruction, "I spake unto you, rising up early and speaking [an idiom expressing urgency and fervency], but ye heard not" (Jer. 7:13; see also 26:5). He, of course, spoke through His prophets, the preachers whom the people ignored.

Haggai is another story—a happy one. His congregation really listened and responded positively to his preaching (1:12–15). Their response was threefold. First, they obeyed. Most significantly, they recognized the words of the prophet to be the very voice of God speaking. Haggai was "the LORD's messenger in the LORD's message" (1:13). What Paul said of the Thessalonians, Haggai could say about Zerubbabel, Joshua, and the remnant of the people: "For this cause also thank we God without ceasing, because, when ye received the word of God which ye heard of us, ye received it not as the word of men, but as it is in truth, the word of God" (1 Thess. 2:13). Obeying God's commandments is evidence of loving Him (1 John 5:3). Loving Him is evidence of correct priorities. Self-interests were giving way to kingdom work.

Second, Haggai's congregation feared the Lord. Consciousness of the Lord's presence with them warranted the fear (1:13). Fearing the Lord is at the heart of true religion and affects both worship and behavior. It is the mind-set of serious and true religion, affecting all of life. To fear the

Lord is simply to live being aware of God, factoring Him into every circumstance and situation of life, living in the conscious sense that God is real. To be overwhelmed with the sense of God's reality puts everything else in perspective; it is a corrective to skewed and misplaced priorities. It motivates behavior that is pleasing to Him.

Third, the congregation became doers of the word, and not hearers only (1:14; see James 1:22). It was not Haggai's eloquence, passion, or logic alone that generated the positive response among the leaders and people; it was the Lord who "stirred up the spirit of Zerubbabel...Joshua...and the spirit of all the remnant of the people." The Hebrew word translated "to stir" means to excite, to arouse, to put in motion. The "spirit" of the people refers to the mind or disposition. Haggai's preaching brought conviction, but when the Lord so moved the people, "they came and did work in the house of the LORD of hosts, their God." Haggai's preaching was the means God used to achieve His end. This is an example of what Paul said in Philippians 2:13: "For it is God which worketh in you both to will and to do of his good pleasure." That the congregation's active response was the consequence of the Lord's exciting them is a reminder of how essential it is for God's power to accompanying the preaching of His Word (see the vivid illustration in Ezekiel's sermon to the dry bones in Ezekiel 37).

But the point is that through Haggai's preaching and God's empowering, the people regained the lost vision and gave themselves once again to the work. The work had ceased for so long that it was going to take some time to get things ready for production. Haggai preached on the first day of the month, and verse 15 refers to the twenty-fourth day of the same month. This most likely refers to the period of just over three weeks required to gear up for the work, particularly if some of the supplies had been used for the people's personal projects. But they learned the lesson well that it was not about them and that nothing was more important than kingdom work, than putting God first and making His cause preeminent. Here comes the temple. Even better, here comes Christ—one more step toward the fullness of time.

Haggai 1:15b – 2:9 D.T. The Time is Now
4 mos – 520 B.C.
spirit of
Haggai + Spirit are dealing w/ discouragement
1 - Delay – temple in ruins for 60 yrs. In 7 wks
they have not done much to rebuild, work was
demanding and delayed.
2-
3 - despised - Satan sowing seed of discouragement
Resist discouragement:
1 - Be strong in the Lord   2:3-4 Take courage
2 - Fear not v.5 - don't be afraid, fear paralyzes
John 5: man at pool, Do we have skills
to rebuild? Do what you can w/ Lord's help
3 - Work for I am w/you, Emmanuel!
ridicule, " " Sovereign Lord of the earth
4 v.5 My Spirit remains in your midst. Nothing
else matters.-
5 - God gives vision - much grander temple

Knowledge of God will cover the earth.

QUESTIONS

1. What was the principal significance of the Feast of Tabernacles that made it an appropriate celebration at the beginning of temple reconstruction?

2. What is the significance of Zerubbabel's replacing Sheshbazzar as the civil leader?

3. What events led to the people's skewed priorities? What kinds of things happen in your life to distract you from your primary spiritual duties?

4. What was significant about the timing of Haggai's first message?

5. What should you do when there is tension between what you believe and what you experience? How have you typically responded?

6. What were the spiritual implications of the people's stopping work on the temple?

7. What commandment does not putting God first in your life transgress? How heinous is this transgression?

8. How should the response to Haggai's first sermon be a paradigm or pattern for all who hear sermons?

VISION
v.6 – shake the nations – God will . v.7 so treasures of all nations will come in, and God will fill this house w/ glory.
Jesus Christ reflects glory of God.
Will outshine old temple
God will come in all His Glory

5

Appearance Is Not Reality

An old adage counsels not to judge a book by its cover. The same applies to temples: don't judge a temple by its foundation. Things are not always what they appear to be; appearance and reality are not always the same. The response to Haggai's first sermon was positive and prompt. Within the month, work on the temple recommenced; the people had regained their vision. However, before another month passed, the people needed a reassuring word about the temple. The vision was still there, but it was out of focus. God always has a word in season for His people, so on the twenty-first day of the seventh month, Haggai, the Lord's messenger, came with a fresh and appropriate word of reassurance from the Lord to put things in sharp focus (2:1–9). The congregation was the same, but the message was different (2:2). The rebuke of the first sermon transitioned to encouragement in the second. Three thoughts sum up Haggai's reassuring and heartening word: the problem, the pledge, and the prospect.

The Problem

The initial reaction to the temple's foundation was mixed. On the one hand, there was excited joy (Ezra 3:11). On the other hand, there was fretful lamentation, specifically among those who were old enough to remember Solomon's temple (Ezra 3:12). That was the mixed feeling before the Samaritan opposition delayed the work, and it resurfaced soon after the work resumed. This is the problem behind Haggai's question: "Who is left among you that saw this house in her first glory? and how do ye see it now? is it not in your eyes in comparison of it as nothing?" (2:3). Haggai's preaching this message in the seventh month would have been pointed since it was in the seventh month that Solomon had dedicated the first temple (1 Kings 8:2). That anniversary perhaps intensified the sense of disappointment when those who remembered Solomon's temple compared it with the prospect of what the next temple was going to look like. If the foundation was any indication of what was coming, there was no comparison. Solomon's temple was magnificently splendid and world renowned. That is undeniable. Structurally and materially it was going to be impossible to duplicate what Solomon had done; it was better then than it could ever be now or again. That backward look was a potential cause for discouragement as the people thought, what's the use?

Whereas the problem Haggai addressed in his first message was a skewed view of priorities, the problem confronted in his second was a skewed view of service. When the people put themselves first, kingdom work suffered. When they put themselves down, working for the kingdom seemed pointless. They estimated the value of their service by comparing it with someone else's, specifically Solomon's. Comparing self with others is never wise (2 Cor. 10:12), and it is certainly not the measure by which to judge how God views the service that is rendered to Him for the advancement of His kingdom. The people were discouraged because what they saw of their efforts did not seem to measure up to what had been done before.

That kind of "sight" reasoning persists and continues to threaten Christians today. We look at how the Reformers changed the course of history or at what the revival preachers of this or that great awakening accomplished, and then we wonder why our labors comparatively seem to accomplish nothing, or at least so little. Many Christians even look down the pew and convince themselves that in comparison to others they are so deficient in spiritual gifts that there is nothing they can do of any worth in serving the Lord. This reflects a serious misunderstanding about the nature of serving the Lord.

This context suggests some significant and corrective truths to keep in mind regarding this misapprehension about kingdom work. The value of service is not determined by how others serve, by what they do, or by the perceived products of service, but by the sincerity and faithfulness of the heart to do whatever is done to God's glory out of gratitude for grace. God distributes gifts according to His sovereign pleasure (1 Cor. 12:4–11)—all in His providence to get the job done. Some jobs are big and some are small, but all are essential. Addressing the same concern, Zechariah will tell us that even holding the measuring line—a task requiring no skill—brings joy to God when done in kingdom work (Zech. 4:10).

It helps as well to remember that the purpose of service is not to enrich God or to impress Him with uniqueness or some special talent. After all, the silver and gold belong to the Lord (Hag. 2:8), so what could we possibly give that would enhance or augment His infinite riches? Neither do we have to devise some novel way to advance His cause. Remember the inventory of gifts the twelve tribes of Israel offered to the Lord in supplying the tabernacle. Remarkably, in Numbers 7 Moses records the gifts brought on twelve successive days by each of the twelve tribes, and every tribe brought exactly the same thing. The point was not so much what they brought, but that they brought and rendered their gifts to the Lord. The point is not to worry about what others do, but just to do what the Lord requires. So in addition to heart sincerity, the value of service will be determined by conformity to the will and purpose of God.

Now back to Haggai. The foundation of the temple under reconstruction was not as impressive as the foundation of Solomon's temple. So what!

The Pledge

God pledged His abiding presence with the people and expected them to respond positively to the promise (2:4–5). The thrice-repeated statement "saith the LORD" (2:4) is a technical expression used for prophetic utterances or oracles—literally, "the utterance of the Lord." The statement itself and its repetition are means of reinforcing the absolute certainty of the declaration.

The Lord pledges His presence twice. The first expression, "I *am* with you" (2:4, italics added), is a verbless clause, the tense of which is specifically undesignated. The temporal ambiguity is itself significant since it could mean, "I *was, am,* or *will be* with you." God is assuring them that He has been with them and will continue to be with them even as He is with them at that very moment. His presence is constant. The second expression, "My spirit remaineth among you" (2:5), highlights the same truth. The Hebrew literally says, "My spirit is standing in your midst." The verb "is standing" is a participle, which expresses the notion of "continual uninterrupted exercise of activity" (so says *Gesenius' Hebrew Grammar*, paragraph 116a, my favorite Hebrew grammar). "To stand" is the idea of standing still or staying. So without interruption, God's Spirit has stood by His people.

Even stronger and more convincing than the grammar is the Lord's explicit declaration that this pledged presence is "according to the word that I covenanted with you when ye came out of Egypt" (2:5). This translation reflects the Hebrew idiom for making a covenant, which literally reads, "the word which I cut with you." "Cutting a covenant" would be the full expression and most likely alludes to the ceremonial cutting in half of a calf; the covenant parties would pass between the parts to ratify the agreement (see Gen. 15:9–17; Jer. 34:18–19). Thus, the Lord's presence is based on a covenant promise that dates to the inception of national existence, the exodus from Egypt. Significantly, the Lord made the same promise to the generation that first erected the tabernacle, the then-symbolic structure of God's presence: "And I will dwell among the children of Israel, and will be their God. And they shall know that I

am the LORD their God, that brought them forth out of the
land of Egypt, that I may dwell among them: I am the LORD
their God" (Ex. 29:45–46). Now, many years later, the Lord
confirms to the generation commissioned with rebuilding
the temple, the symbolic structure of God's presence, that
nothing had changed. He was still with His people.

As God's presence was associated with the tabernacle
and then with the temple, so it is with the current manifestation of the temple, the very body of believers: "For ye are
the temple of the living God; as God hath said, I will dwell
in them, and walk in them; and I will be their God, and
they shall be my people" (2 Cor. 6:16; see also 1 Cor. 6:19).
God is still with His people.

Being conscious of God's presence affects both attitude
and behavior. On the basis of God's pledged presence, the
Lord issues three separate commands to mark His expectations for people: be strong, work, do not fear. The first and
third concern attitude or mind-set (exercises of faith), and
the middle gets right to the point of behavior.

The first imperative, "be strong," is repeated three
times, personally to Zerubbabel, to Joshua, and to all the
people of the land (2:4). The sense of the verb refers to
mental rather than physical strength, the idea being to
have courage or be courageous. This was not a matter of
self-confidence, but rather confidence in the Lord. Being
strong, therefore, was a matter of faith. They were to remain
resolute and determined to fulfill the task at hand regardless of hindrances. Because God was with them, they had
the means to withstand any opposition, even that which
would come from within.

The second imperative is "work" (2:4). God expected them to act in response to His word of promise. This command needs no exposition; it is clear and unmistakable. They were to be doers of the word, not just hearers. Given God's presence, there was no excuse for not getting the job done.

The third command is negative, a prohibition: "Fear ye not" (2:5). Not to fear is an expression of faith; it is walking contrary to sight. Invariably when the Lord tells His people not to be afraid, they are in circumstances that are scary, dangerous, or threatening. From every natural perspective they would have every right to fear. But faith is not a natural response. In one way or another, what is feared determines behavior. This is why it is so vital to fear the Lord rather than man or circumstance. Faith is being more aware of God, who is invisible to physical sight, than all the things that are so plainly in view. Awareness of the reality of God's presence dispels every other reason to fear. The psalmist expresses this beautifully with words that have become so familiar: "Yea, though I walk through the valley of the shadow of death, I will fear no evil: for thou art with me" (Ps. 23:4). The "valley of the shadow of death" literally refers to a place of deep darkness where a lot of scary things would lurk and threaten. But because of the sense of God's presence, David was not afraid of any potential danger. That is the application of God's presence that Haggai impressed upon the people. They had already faced some fearful opposition that had paralyzed them, causing the work to cease. In all likelihood, fearful things would lie ahead as well, but living in the sense of God's presence would keep them working regardless.

The Prospect

The last point of Haggai's sermon brings us to the title of the chapter: appearance is not reality. Haggai set before the people the prospect of great things to come. They had assumed the best was behind them; Haggai declared the best was yet to be. It appeared that the architecture and accoutrements of the temple-under-construction were going to be inferior to the temple that had been destroyed. That, indeed, was true enough. However, in contrast to appearance, the reality was that the rebuilt temple would be far more glorious than the first, and they had the Lord's word on it: "The glory of this latter house shall be greater than of the former, saith the LORD of hosts" (2:9). There is more to reality than meets the eye.

The Lord was about to interrupt all creation in order to accomplish His special purpose: "Yet once, it is a little while, and I will shake the heavens, and the earth, and the sea, and the dry land; and I will shake all nations" (2:6–7). The language is startling. On the one hand, it resembles language associated with theophany. A theophany is a special manifestation or appearance of God in some symbolic form, like the cloud or pillar of fire present during the wilderness experience. For instance, Isaiah expresses his desire that God would rend the heavens and come down, causing mountains to melt and nations to tremble (Isa. 64:1–2). Similarly, Joel associates a quaking earth and trembling heavens as an attendant circumstance to the Day of the Lord, a special time when God intervenes directly and unmistakably into the affairs of time (Joel 2:10–11). Significantly, the preacher in the book of Hebrews alludes to Haggai 2:6 to exhort faithfulness to God's immovable kingdom, having issued a warning against rejecting Jesus (Heb. 12:25–28). The point is clear that nothing remains unaffected when God comes down, and Haggai is about to reveal the most stupendous descension of God in all of history: the incarnation of the Son of God. The incarnation changed everything.

Haggai predicts the incarnation in these terms: "The desire of all nations shall come" (2:7). I've indicated my interpretation up front, but I must acknowledge that not all agree that this refers to the coming of Jesus. This gets a bit complicated, but I will try to be simple and offer just a synopsis of the issue. The contention surrounds the referent of the word "desire," whether it is impersonal or personal. The word, sometimes translated "pleasant," conveys the idea of that which is desirable or regarded as precious, and in the Old Testament refers to both people (for instance, Saul in 1 Sam. 9:20; Jehoram in 2 Chron. 21:20; and the promised Seed of the woman in Dan. 11:37) and things (for instance, houses in Ezek. 26:12; and vessels in Hos. 13:15). The meaning of the word, then, does not provide a conclusive argument one way or the other.

The grammar adds another point of question. The noun "desire" is the subject of the clause. It is singular, but the verb is plural, suggesting that "desire" should be understood as a collective noun, which simply means it is plural in meaning although singular in form: "the desirable things of all the nations will come." This would mean that the precious things or wealth of the nations would come to the temple, almost as though the Gentiles would be plundered to furnish the temple. There are statements that would seem to support this notion: "The forces [literally, wealth] of the Gentiles shall come unto thee" (Isa. 60:5); "Ye shall eat the riches of the Gentiles" (Isa. 61:6); "The wealth of all the heathen round about shall be gathered together, gold, and silver, and apparel, in great abundance" (Zech. 14:14). Just as the Israelites "plundered" the Egyptians at the exodus and most likely used some of that spoil in the building of the tabernacle (see Ex. 12:35–36 and 35:22), the Gentiles would supply the goods for this temple.

There is obviously an undeniable truth that Gentiles will serve and be subjects of God's kingdom (Rev. 21:24, 26). For that we can be most thankful. But I'm not convinced that the ultimate subjection of the Gentiles, either by rod or by grace, is what Haggai has in focus in this context. After all, since the silver and gold belong to the Lord (2:8), He doesn't need anyone to bankroll the project. The glory with which He will fill this temple has nothing to do with silver or gold. Verse 8 is a clue that we are not to interpret the desired thing in verse 7 materially.

This brings us back to my initial remark that the statement points to the incarnation. It is Christ, the Desire of all Nations, whose presence will come "suddenly" to this temple (Mal. 3:1) and who will fill the house with glory. The tabernacle in the wilderness and Solomon's splendid temple were overshadowed, engulfed, by the *shekinah* glory cloud of God's presence. That was remarkable. But this temple, outwardly inferior, would be graced with the immediate and physical presence of God Incarnate. That would be incomparable glory.

That Christ would be designated as the Desire of Nations has significant gospel implications. Although Jesus descended through the lineage of Israel (Rom. 9:4–5), the promise of the Messiah has never been uniquely a Jewish promise. Entering humanity as the Seed of woman (Gen. 3:15), Christ was to be the source of blessing for the entire world (Gen. 12:3; 2 Sam. 7:19—"is this the manner of man" is literally "this is the revelation for humanity"). So in a covenant declaration, Haggai refers to the Desire of Nations. It makes good gospel sense.

But that leaves the grammatical question about the plural verb. Confessedly, it is unusual since Hebrew typically maintains a strict agreement between subjects and verbs both in terms of gender and number. I cannot be dogmatic, but here's my explanation. Although I believe "desire" has a singular referent, Christ, it is a pregnant or full construction that encompasses all that Christ is and has. He is man's most prized possession, as God having intrinsic worth. To have Christ is to have everything. There is a theological sense in which Christ, as the Mediator and Redeemer of God's elect, cannot be without His people. So to express the multiple components, complexities, and inclusiveness of His messiahship, the plural verb is used. Grammatically, "desire" has a single referent, but it is collective in view of all the things included in Him. That explanation satisfies me. Sometimes theology takes precedence over traditional grammar.

I prefer the messianic interpretation of verse 7, but either way the lesson of the second sermon is clear: God had a purpose for His people greater than their perceptions. The second temple would have greater glory because the Desire was coming. What appeared to them was not the reality of God's purpose. The hope of something greater was to motivate and encourage them to work.

The applications of this truth are significant and helpful for us who are so prone to allow appearance and perceptions to rule. Learn the lesson that, particularly in the spiritual realm, appearance and reality are often not the same. The reality is that we are blessed right now with all spiritual blessings in the heavenly places in Christ Jesus (Eph. 1:3). It may not seem like that when we look around, but the reality is that we are now, in a sense, in heaven in union with Christ. That is profound, and the experience and enjoyment of it ought to be our desire. Since the word "desire" includes the sense of treasure, it means that Christ should be our prized possession. If He is our treasure, our heart will be with Him (Matt. 6:19–21; Col. 3:1–2).

5.14

Haggai 2:10-19 Josh Squires   The Time is Now.

1 – context
2 – conviction
3 – consolation v. 18-19
– literary - God shows mercy to his people
  who have repented, even BAD people
  when people trust + obey
  historical – God leaves His people at the temple,
– ceremony – is holiness contagious? v. 12 don't become
  holy by going to temple. Holiness is heart thing)
  Holy not just being in temple. The temple →

QUESTIONS

1. Why is it never wise to compare self with others?

2. What is the image behind the Hebrew idiom for making a covenant?

3. How do believers today experience God's presence?

4. What does it mean to be strong spiritually?

5. In what sense is not being afraid an expression of faith?

6. Think of instances that illustrate the spiritual truth that appearance and reality are not the same.

Is holiness contagious?
Defiled in hearts broken down temple for
16 years they've done nothing.
2 Sam 7:5. Temple window into people's
heart. Don't worry about cares of the
world, seek first the kingdom of God
Haggai was saying this
Promise of faith v.19 "I will bless you"
Blessing for defiled people
Blessing = anything that gets you closer to
God that I will be His people
Only one who can put me at peace
w/ God = Jesus Christ = that's blessed

6

Blessing Starts Now

For the repatriates commissioned with the rebuilding of the temple, 9/24/520 BC was a special day. On this day Haggai preached his final two messages (2:10, 20). But the end of Haggai's inspired career marked the beginning of a special administration of divine benediction. To put it simply, the Lord said on this day, "Blessing starts now" (2:19).

In some ways, the first of Haggai's final two sermons, although ending with the announcement of commenced blessing, seems out of place. Three months earlier work on the temple resumed (1:14–15), and there is no evidence of any hiatus in the work during this time frame. It appeared that all was well. Yet the tone and terms of the opening point of this third sermon are sternly negative, similar in both tone and terms to Haggai's first message delivered before the work recommenced. Notwithstanding, what may seem on the surface to be out of place must be right on target since it is inspired, the record of the very mind of God. It was something Haggai's congregation needed to hear. Indeed, this sermon develops two key thoughts—two things to consider or, literally, to set the heart upon (2:15, 18, note the double occurrence of the imperative framing the verse). They are thoughts to ponder even when engaged in doing the work of the kingdom: sin is bad; blessing is good.

Sin Is Bad

Since the people had responded positively to his first sermon and resumed work on the temple, Haggai reminds them in this third sermon of the cost and consequences of neglecting the work of the Lord for their own interests. Remembering how bad things were when their priorities were skewed should have been an incentive to avoid God's displeasure again. Before I consider how Haggai argues the badness of sin, I'm going to comment on the part of the sermon that suggests this to be a retrospective warning.

Verses 14–17 imply this retrospective look, although the tenses used in verse 14 suggest otherwise. After describing the infectious nature of uncleanness, Haggai said, "So *is* this people, and so *is* this nation…and so *is* every work…. That which they offer there *is* unclean." The present tense would seem to indicate this to be an indictment of the people who were engaged in the temple construction. Note, however, that every "is" is in italics in the King James Version, a technique employed by the translators to indicate when they supplied something that was not directly in the original text. In Hebrew, each of these clauses is actually verbless, which requires readers to determine the actual time from the context. Grammatically, the statements could read "was," "is," or "will be." Given how closely the following verses parallel the scene in the first sermon and that they were to consider the time before a stone was laid on stone (2:15), it appears that every "is" in verse 14 should be "was," referring to the previous status.

The similarities between Haggai 2:16–17 and 1:6–11 suggest the prophet is pointing his finger back to when the people were living for themselves, trapped in life's proverbial rat race. Everything they did to get ahead proved futile (2:16), and their failed labors traced directly to God: "I smote you...in all the labours of your hands" (2:17). The language is reminiscent of the covenant curses delineated in Deuteronomy 28:22. Both Moses and Haggai made it unmistakably clear that it doesn't pay to disobey. Yet, notwithstanding the evidences of divine displeasure and discipline in their spiritual insensitivity, the people failed to see the connection between their poor productivity and their behavior before the Lord. Therefore, they did not turn to the Lord (2:17), or, it might read more literally, "nonexistence of you to me," a way of expressing that they were behaving without reference to the Lord. That's the flip side of their living with reference to themselves, their skewed priorities. But, happily, they did come to their senses and got back to kingdom work. Apparently the prophet's preaching accomplished what providence alone did not (1:12), which testifies to God's patience and grace in sending His prophets with His word to interpret His acts. But human nature is such that it is easy to revert back to the old ways at the first hint of difficulty or when things don't go quite as expected. So Haggai issues the warning about how bad sin is and how severe its consequences.

In the first part of his third sermon, Haggai addresses the badness of sin by appealing to the priests for instruction

regarding the Levitical laws of cleanness and uncleanness
(2:11–13). The laws of cleanness and uncleanness are delineated particularly in Leviticus 11–15 and Deuteronomy 14.
These regulations were important components in the ceremonial law and provide a great illustration of the conflict
that every believer faces by living in the world. These sections of the Old Testament seem strange, and it is easy to
get bogged down or sidetracked in trying to interpret many
of the details. Notwithstanding the specific difficulties in
discerning what was clean or unclean, there was an obvious
lesson that God was teaching His people, one that we must
learn as well: fellowship with God demands purity. Whatever else may have been the point in all the regulations, it
was clear that to be unclean precluded participation in the
rituals and ceremonies of worship. Therefore, Israel was to
be vigilant in avoiding whatever would produce uncleanness. They were to walk circumspectly because there were
so many things around them that could rob them of fellowship with God. That remains true for us today.

But Haggai zeros in on one aspect of the laws to make
his point: sin is infectious. Something clean that touches
something unclean does not render the unclean clean
(2:12), but something unclean, by simple contact, con-
taminates the clean (2:13). There is no such thing as almost
clean; any dirt makes something unclean. Rubbing a greasy
rag on a clean shirt spoils the shirt. Likewise, wiping up
an oil spill with a clean shirt may smear the oil, making
its appearance fade, but in the process the shirt is soiled
and ruined. Sin is horribly contagious—a common warning throughout Scripture. The Preacher warned that just as

dead flies can spoil the whole vat of perfume, so a little folly is capable of ruining a reputation (Eccl. 10:1). Similarly, the apostle cautioned that since a little leaven leavens the whole lump, it is vital to get rid of the old leaven (1 Cor. 5:6–7).

The principal application of Haggai's warning is to deal with sin and to do so before its effects spread to others. The happy truth is that whatever the cause or occasion of the uncleanness, there was always an appropriate sacrifice to address the uncleanness and restore to fellowship and usefulness. This is the blood rule summarized in Hebrews 9:22: "Almost all things are by the law purged with blood; and without shedding of blood is no remission." This points directly to the sacrifice of Christ, who "once in the end of the world hath…appeared to put away sin" (Heb. 9:26). Although even the best we do is imperfect and tainted with sin, the blood of Jesus avails to keep on cleansing us from all sin (1 John 1:7). There is a solution to the badness of sin.

Blessing Is Good

The occurrence of "consider" (literally, "set your heart") at both the beginning and end of Haggai 2:18 marks the transition from the warning of curse to the prospect of blessing. Within the verbal frame is the record of the temple's foundation being laid, the evidence that the people had been engaged in the mandated kingdom work. The work was not done, but it was in progress. In the light of that progress, the people had every right to hope with eager expectancy that things would be better. God's displeasure with the skewed priorities had been bad; His blessing for their realigned priorities had to be good.

That hope for divine blessing was not just the presumption that God owed the people something for their efforts and labor, but rather it was founded on God's own word of promise. Moses not only delineated the curses for disobedience, some of which they had so specifically experienced, he also outlined the blessings for obedience (Deut. 28:1–14). Enjoying the blessings was their expectation as much as enduring the curses had been their experience. Haggai reinforced that expectation when he recorded the Lord's direct word to this people: "From this day will I bless you" (2:19). It appeared that things were about to get better.

This raises the question as to what blessing looks like. The question and assertions of Haggai 2:19 suggest that the appearance of blessing may be contrary to expectation. This verse is not without difficulty and suffers from multiple interpretations regarding the time frame and referents. It is beyond my scope to address them all since this is not a critical commentary. But one thing is clear on the surface: the land was not at that moment yielding any produce. There was neither seed in reserve to plant nor fruit on vines or trees to harvest. But in the midst of what appeared to be barrenness, the Lord announced the certainty of His blessing. Divine blessing and favor are not defined by stuff. To limit God's blessing to tangible things generates a motive for service that it is aimed at getting stuff rather than pleasing the Lord. That is materialism, just another form of the selfishness that caused their trouble in the first place.

The announcement of commenced blessing, which was the evidence of divine favor, constitutes the essence of real blessing. To know that God is pleased is beyond words to express. Yet about eighty-five years earlier, Habakkuk, on the eve of the front end of the captivity, said it well: "Although the fig tree shall not blossom, neither shall fruit be in the vines; the labour of the olive shall fail, and the fields shall yield no meat; the flock shall be cut off from the fold, and there shall be no herd in the stalls: yet I will rejoice in the LORD, I will joy in the God of my salvation" (3:17–18).

Blessing is good when the blessing is the Lord. That is the essence of this conclusion of Haggai's third sermon.

QUESTIONS

1. Why does Haggai's third sermon seem to be out of place?

2. What is the main point of application in the third sermon?

3. What is the principal lesson in the laws of cleanness and uncleanness?

4. What is the blood rule, and how does it apply to Christians?

5. If God's blessing is not to be defined in terms of material prosperity, how do we know we are experiencing divine blessing?

7

The Best Is Yet to Be

On 9/24/520 BC, Haggai had a busy day. He preached twice, and his second message marked the end of his prophetic career, at least his writing career. Haggai's final inspired sermon sounded a note of triumph. His first sermon of the day announced the beginning of blessing; his final sermon declared its consummation. The prospect of blessing was good, but the best was yet to be.

The book of Haggai ends with the final triumph of the kingdom of Christ. That was most encouraging news and assured the temple workers that no part of kingdom work is futile. The construction of the temple was an integral component in preparing the way for the fullness of time when Christ would come, but it was just a part of God's overall and unfailing plan. Sometimes involvement in a part clouds the vision of the whole, and discouragement sets in when all that is seen seems so insignificant. Haggai assured the people that every task in the work of the kingdom, even laying a foundation and stacking stones, was advancing step by step to the culmination of God's unfailing redemptive plan. Keeping the end in sight would keep the present in focus. The final word seemed too good to be true, but it was certainly true.

Significantly and almost paradoxically, Haggai directed his final word to Zerubbabel, the civil authority charged with supervising the temple reconstruction. Although he was the civil leader and even of the tribe of Judah and a descendant of David, he was not the king. David's throne was still vacant, and Zerubbabel's "royal-less-ness" appeared to affirm the end of any functional kingly dynasty. Persia had been providentially directed to provide aid and protection for the temple project, but it was nonetheless a foreign power with jurisdiction over Israel. After Persia would come Greece, and then Rome. When Haggai spoke to Zerubbabel, Israel faced centuries of foreign domination. When the scribes and Pharisees told Jesus that they "were never in bondage to any man" (John 8:33), you have to wonder where they learned history or through what lens they interpreted current events. From what could be seen, it did not seem like Christ's kingdom was marching on.

But in reality it was. Years earlier in his great virgin birth prophecy, Isaiah had predicted that when Immanuel would come, the land would be under foreign domination (suggested by the imagery in Isa. 7:17–25). The state of affairs caused by Persia, Greece, and Rome was all part of God's plan. The throne, therefore, was not to be Zerubbabel's, but the One to whom it truly belonged was on His way (see Ezek. 21:27). It was always part of the design of predictive prophecy to bring the future to bear on the present. If Zerubbabel and those he led would be convinced of the certainty of what God would do, they would be motivated to fulfill their duty even in the light of the perceived small-ness and insignificance of their efforts. So to hearten the people to progress from the temple's foundation to its cap-stone, Haggai declared that the kingdoms of this world would fail and that the kingdom of Christ would prevail. He develops this assurance with two principal points high-lighting the divine conquest and the divine certitude.

The Divine Conquest

Earthly kingdoms come and go; that's the stuff of history. Even though the course and destiny of nations may have political, economic, military, or religious rationalizations, the reality is that there is one throne secluded from natural sight that governs every shift and struggle for dominance on earth from the beginning of time—God's throne. That was Daniel's testimony before he revealed and interpreted Nebuchadnezzar's dream that overviewed in preview the movement of kingdoms from Babylon to Rome and beyond: "Blessed be the name of God for ever and ever: for wisdom and might are his: and he changeth the times and the seasons: he removeth kings, and setteth up kings" (Dan. 2:20–21). Effecting transitions of human power and author-ity was and remains the ordinary work of divine providence.

Repeating the divine declaration from 2:6, Haggai points to a drastic event beyond the normal operations of providence with the startling declaration of God's voice: "I will shake the heavens and the earth" (2:21). A time is com-ing when the behind-the-scenes works of providence give way to a divinely manifested interruption of the normal course of circumstance. This is the language of theophany and is severe and inclusive. The severity is expressed by the participle construction translated "I will shake." The verb means literally "to cause to shudder or quake." By using the participle, which has a tense or time that is contextual, the Lord declares that with uninterrupted and unhindered activity He will cause all creation to shudder. Referring to the heavens and the earth is a literary device to express the idea of inclusiveness—hence, all creation. None will be able to stay His hand, and none will be able to escape, as there will be no place to hide. The consequences of this divine shaking are unavoidable. Interestingly, Hebrews 12:25–29 alludes to Haggai 2:21 as a warning to all who refuse to hear and heed God's word in the gospel. In contrast to the rejecters of God's word are believers, who have a part in God's immovable kingdom. Although the application points differ a bit, Hebrews and Haggai point to the same kingdom. One way or another, the caution is not to trifle with or ignore the Lord, for "our God is a consuming fire" (Heb. 12:29).

Haggai's focal point of application for his immediate audience concerns God's conquest and subjugation of earthly kingdoms, all those that appeared to be obstacles to the coming of Christ's kingdom. In view particularly are the kingdoms of the heathen (2:22). This does not refer to primitive pagans, but to the Gentile nations of the world that, according to Psalm 2:1–3, are agitated and restless against Jehovah and His Messiah and so plot and scheme of ways to tear off the fetters and bonds of divine control. Haggai makes it clear that in spite of their plans and efforts to throw off God's authority, they are doomed and destined to failure. Rather, in verse 22 the Lord declares, "I will overthrow the throne of kingdoms." The throne is the symbol of authority, which the Lord will literally "turn upside down." In addition, the Lord "will destroy the strength of the kingdoms." If "throne" represents authority in the abstract, "strength" refers to the active ability to use force to achieve ends. The specific form of the verb "to destroy" suggests the deliberate compulsion of the action. With relentless and irresistible determination and resolve, the Lord will destroy, rendering useless and neutralizing the power of the Gentiles.

What is stated in principle will be executed by direct divine causation and by indirect human manipulation. The Lord will overturn the thrones and neutralize power directly by turning upside down the war chariots along with those riding in them. This goes beyond just a limited reference to chariots; rather, by metonymy (association between words) or, more specifically, by synecdoche (part for the whole), it refers to disarmament in general, regardless of the particular weapons. The Lord will decimate the armies of the Gentiles. He is the direct cause: "I will turn upside down." Yet, He can realize His will in secondary ways if He sees fit. In a tragically comical scene, the Lord describes the cavalry ("the horses and their riders") as falling down, "every one by the sword of his brother." It is a picture of anarchy, chaos, panic, and confusion as the Gentile armies fight against themselves. Perhaps this is in part what generates the holy laughter from heaven that David described in Psalm 2:4: "He that sitteth in the heavens shall laugh: the LORD shall have them in derision." The kingdoms of this world that set themselves against God and His people cannot prevail; that is the bottom line.

The Divine Certitude

Significantly, David's kingdom theology expressed in Psalm 2 parallels the logic and outline of Haggai's argument. After God speaks to the nations "in his wrath" and vexes them "in his sore displeasure" (Ps. 2:5; equating to Hag. 2:22), He confirms, "Yet have I set my king upon my holy hill of Zion" (Ps. 2:6). Nothing could frustrate the reign of Christ, and the certain reign of Christ was the guarantee of the fall of every other kingdom. So, after announcing the fall of earthly kingdoms, Haggai shifted to the certainty of the coming Messiah (2:23). The certitude of this prophetic utterance is heightened because it comes from the Lord of Hosts. This divine title identifies the Lord as the commander in chief of armies. Everything in creation is at His disposal and under His command to accomplish His purpose. The repetition of "saith the LORD of hosts" at the beginning and end of Haggai 2:23 frames the divine oracle with assurance of success. There could be no doubt regarding the certitude of this promise. Messiah was going to come.

Obviously, I need to explain because there does not appear to be any reference to Messiah in verse 23, at least at first read. But Christ is indeed in view. So I will make a statement and then justify it before making the point of the text. Here is the statement: God designates Zerubbabel, the civil leader in David's line, as a type of the coming Messiah.

Here is the justification of what I'm saying. First, let me define what I mean by *type*. A type is a real historical

person, event, or thing used as an object lesson or symbol
to foreshadow or predict the actual, future realization or
fulfillment of the pictured truth. Simply stated, a type is a
picture-prophecy. An antitype is the future realization to
which the type points; it is the fulfillment of the picture-
prophecy. Types are divinely intended analogies whose
salient points not only correspond to but also predict the
antitype, the main topic of the revelation. Types do not
exist just because someone thinks he discerned something
in the text that reminds him about Christ when he thinks
about it hard enough. I want to be very clear that typology is not an interpretation technique that we arbitrarily
impose on an Old Testament text in an effort to rescue that
text for Christian relevance. Types are divinely intended,
and to miss recognizing them is to misinterpret the text.
God is saying, "Look at this [in this case, Zerubbabel] to
learn something about that [in this case, Messiah]."

Second, although typology is not an arbitrary hermeneutical option forced on the text, certain rules and
guidelines of hermeneutics should govern the interpretation
of types. Two issues are on the surface: how to recognize or
identify a type, and how to determine the significance of
the type once it is identified. Two points, in particular, will
give some help in identifying the type in this text.

1. *Keep the antitype in focus.* To focus on the type alone is
to miss the point. Interestingly, one way the New Testament
refers to types is by calling them shadows (Col. 2:17). A
shadow exists because there is a real substance that casts
the shadow. The normal reaction to a shadow is to look

for the object that casts it. The only reason that God used shadows or types in the Old Testament dispensation is that Christ was the substance, the reality, of what He wanted men to see. The normal and expected reaction to the Old Testament shadows was to look for Christ. Ultimately, the substance defines the shadow, not the other way around. So the more we know about Christ, the more we will be able to recognize Him, even in the shadowy forms and picture prophecies. It is messianic theology that must limit identifying types of Christ. We should always read the Scripture being on "Christ alert." Something about the picture must in its context be a reminder of something God has previously revealed about His plan and purpose of salvation in and through the promised Seed. When we see something that bears some resemblance or congruity to what we know about Christ, pause.

2. *Know the kinds of things that God used as types.* Old Testament types fall into three categories: people, things, and events. I want to emphasize that all were actual, historical entities and occurrences. Types were not simply hypothetical illustrations; they were real. Certain people were types of Christ not because of their personalities or character traits, but by virtue of their office. Certain things or objects were types of Christ by virtue of their function. When we observe that a thing received special attention or focus in contexts of ritual, redemption, or deliverance, we have good reason for plugging in what we know about Christ to see if there is some correspondence. Certain events were types of Christ's work by virtue of either their agent or

their accomplishment. In a real and important sense, all the events recorded in the Old Testament are integral elements in the history of redemption, and, therefore, in one way or another they prepare the way for the coming of Christ, the climax of redemptive history. Yet certain epochal events stand out as particularly illustrative of the redemptive work of God through Christ. God's pointing to Zerubbabel, His servant, as a signet underscores the divine certitude of His word by directing attention to the certain coming of Christ, the climax of His unfailing plan and purpose.

In Haggai 2:23, a couple of things should give us pause and direct our sight from Zerubbabel, the shadow, to Christ, the substance. The statement "in that day" is technical jargon designating the Day of the Lord, a special, direct, divine intervention into the affairs of time. Here it refers to the events of 2:21–22, so the temporal context, pointing to that future, climactic shaking of the heavens and earth, precludes Zerubbabel from being the principal topic, yet points to Christ, who is most assuredly the central figure in that consummation. Also, since the signet is associated with royalty and Zerubbabel never attained royal status, the context points to the certain King to come. So if we keep the antitype in focus, we can see Christ in Zerubbabel, the shadowy figure of Him who was certain to come.

In Haggai 2:23 the type is twofold: Zerubbabel as a messianic person and the signet as a messianic object. Although he was not officially a king, Zerubbabel served as the civil authority who led and supervised the people in their kingdom work. In his capacity as God's servant in that role of leadership, he pictured the ideal Servant to come. The signet was a symbol of the authority and privilege belonging to the royal office. When God removed the signet from Jehoiachin (Jer. 22:24), it appeared that all hope of a Davidic kingdom was gone: "Thus saith the LORD, Write ye this man childless, a man that shall not prosper in his days: for no man of his seed shall prosper, sitting upon the throne of David, and ruling any more in Judah" (Jer. 22:30). God stripped Jehoiachin of honor and excluded his descendants from sitting on the throne. One reason Zerubbabel could not assume the throne was he was a descendant of Jehoiachin (see 1 Chron. 3:17–19). But the signet was a symbol guaranteeing the unconditional certainty of God's covenant with David that his "greater Son" would rule nonetheless.

The Lord kept His covenant word to David, transferring kingship to another of his sons and vouchsafing the promise that was realized in Jesus. Compare the genealogies of Jesus in Matthew 1 and Luke 3 to see how both the sentence on the house of Jehoiachin and promise of a Davidic king were fulfilled. Matthew traces the legal line of Jesus from Joseph back to David through Solomon, whereas Luke traces his actual line from Mary back to David through Nathan, Solomon's brother. Everything was working unfailingly according to plan.

The Babylonian captivity marked what appeared to be the end of the Davidic dynasty, but in reality it was preparation for its ultimate manifestation. Ezekiel records God's purpose at the beginning of the exilic period: "Remove the diadem, and take off the crown.... I will overturn, overturn, overturn, it: and it shall be no more, until he come whose right it is; and I will give it him" (Ezek. 21:26–27;

see also Shiloh ["to whom it belongs"] in Gen. 49:10). Now, at the end of the captivity, Haggai records God telling the people "not to worry." Zerubbabel was designated as the signet, the guarantee that everything was on track for the rightful King.

There could be no better way for Haggai to end his series of sermons than with the assurance that Christ was coming. Over five hundred years remained before He would come, but He was coming, and the best was yet to be.

QUESTIONS

1. How was Haggai's final sermon relevant when the people would not themselves see the fulfillment?

2. What about the imagery of Isaiah 7:17–25 suggests that the land would be under foreign domination when Immanuel would come? (Hint: The answer is in Isaiah, not in my discussion.)

3. How does Haggai's prediction of divine conquest differ from the ordinary works of providence?

4. What psalm parallels Haggai's argument in the last sermon? In what way does it parallel Haggai's argument?

5. Explain why Zerubbabel is a type of Christ. Factor in the discussion of types.

6. What does it mean to be on "Christ alert," and how should that affect your reading of any portion in the Old Testament?

7. Explain how the signet of Haggai 2:23 pointed to Christ.

8. Meditate on how Haggai's final prediction concerning Christ should impact your thinking and living.

—PART 3—

Zechariah: The Idealist

Facts about Zechariah

Zechariah was Haggai's younger contemporary. Called at the same time to address the same people concerning the same issue, the two prophets conducted their ministries differently, although their messages and objectives were the same. Haggai evinced the realism of age, whereas Zechariah displayed the idealism of youth. But their age was not ultimately a factor, for both were inspired by the same Spirit to preach the messages given to them from the same God. That God used equally two preachers with different personalities and styles is encouraging. Too often success or usability in kingdom work is defined in terms of personalities rather than faithfulness to God's call. How God distributes His servants in His vineyard and what particular abilities He grants are His business. It is encouraging that God uses dissimilar men to serve, as we see in these two prophets. We must do what God calls us to do without comparing ourselves to others.

The Man

Whereas nothing is recorded about Haggai's lineage, the Scripture traces Zechariah's ancestry back two generations.

Zechariah 1:1 identifies him as "the son of Berechiah, the son of Iddo the prophet." That Ezra 5:1 and 6:14 identify him as the son of Iddo is no contradiction since Hebrew often uses the word "son" to refer to even a distant descendant, in this instance a grandson. Ezra's linking Zechariah directly to Iddo was most likely due to Iddo's being better known than Berechiah. Even the genealogy in Nehemiah 12:16 skips Berechiah, going directly from Iddo to Zechariah, not an uncommon phenomenon in ancient genealogies, including those in the Old Testament. According to Nehemiah 12:1–4, Iddo was among the priests that returned to Palestine along with Zerubbabel. Thus, he would have been part of the initial work on the temple and perhaps among those priests and elders who lamented over the temple's foundation (Ezra 3:12; Hag. 2:3). Juxtaposing Iddo and Zechariah provides a touch of symmetry as well. Iddo, the priest, was involved in the initial stages of the temple's reconstruction; Zechariah, the priest by birth and prophet by divine call, was instrumental in seeing the work brought to completion.

It is impossible to know precisely Zechariah's age when he began his prophetic career in 520 BC, but he would have been considerably younger than Haggai, who was most likely part of his grandfather's generation. Although we do not know the date or his age at the time of his death, we do know how he died due to a statement of the Lord Jesus. In His lamentation over Jerusalem "that killest the prophets," Jesus referred to all the blood that was shed "from the blood of righteous Abel unto the blood of Zacharias son of Barachias, whom ye slew between the temple and the altar" (Matt. 23:35–37). By mentioning Abel, the first martyr, and Zechariah, the last of the martyred prophets, Jesus uses a literary device called *merismus* to include all those in between as well. Referring to polar expressions is a way of expressing totality. Jesus makes reference to an event not recorded in the Old Testament but apparently known to those to whom He was preaching. Interestingly, the manner and place of the prophet's death parallels that of another Zechariah, the son of Jehoiada the priest, who was martyred in the temple court during the administration of Joash (2 Chron. 24:20–21). In fact, had Jesus not specified that Barachias was the father of the martyred Zechariah, we would assume He had in mind the instance recorded in 2 Chronicles. Ironically, Zechariah was killed at the very temple that he was instrumental in rebuilding. What caused the people to turn on him we do not know, but that they did is indisputable. Jesus said so, and that settles it.

But before they did, Zechariah had a lengthy ministry spanning approximately fifty years. He dates his first series of messages (chapters 1–6) to the second year of Darius, which corresponds to Ezra's historical record of when both Haggai and Zechariah prophesied (Ezra 4:24; 5:1). This calculates to 520 BC. Zechariah then dates a second series (chapters 7–8) two years later in the fourth year of Darius (518 BC). However, the tone and focus of the message seem to shift in chapters 9–14. These chapters consist of two oracles, each introduced with the assertion "the burden of the word of the LORD" (9:1; 12:1). Zechariah does not date these messages like he did at the beginning, but

reading between the lines and sometimes reading the line
directly (for instance, references to Greece such as in 9:13)
suggest a later date. Most conservatives date this portion of
the prophecy between 480–470 BC. By this time the temple
would have been completed for approximately forty years,
and the people were on their way to the spiritual deadness
that Malachi was going to confront in a few more years.
So it is certainly conceivable that by this time there could
have been some malcontents treacherous enough to kill the
prophet, just as Jesus said.

The Message

Zechariah, whose name declares "the Lord remembers,"
is the great prophet of hope. The seventy-year captivity
was over, but the end of those years did not usher in the
expected blessing and prosperity. Those who had returned
to Israel from Babylon and beyond did so with expectant
hope, but soon faced opposition from the Samaritans, desolation in the land, hard work, and hardships. Hope faded
in the darkness of the difficulties. It seemed as though the
Lord had forgotten.

Just hearing Zechariah's name would have been a
reminder that the Lord had not forgotten. But his message
of encouragement in the midst of all their difficulties went
far beyond his name tag. At the beginning of his ministry,
his agenda was the same as Haggai's—to move the people
to resume their kingdom work of temple reconstruction.
Haggai forthrightly had the people consider their own
ways as he confronted their self-generated problem of
skewed priorities. Zechariah, on the other hand, pointed

them away from themselves and current circumstances to the magnitude of what God had in store for them. The principal theme of Zechariah's message was *hope in God's unfailing purpose.* Hoping in that overarching redemptive plan would give them the heart to live in victory and to serve with diligence. Looking away from the discouraging "now" to the certain and glorious "then" was and remains today the proper perspective of faith.

This future perspective of faith is what the Bible refers to as hope and what describes the thrust of Zechariah's message, even though the word "hope" occurs only once in the prophecy. In 9:12, he addresses the "prisoners of hope," a beautiful designation of those captivated by hope in the multiplied blessings promised by God. This hope may be idealistic, but it is not make-believe. Like all true faith, hope is objective, and the value of faith, even hope as its future focus, depends on the value of its object. Hope, therefore, is not a trembling, hesitant, cross-your-fingers wish that everything will be okay in the end. On the contrary, it is a confident expectation that God's promises cannot be anything but true. Hope is the trademark of faith, and experience of hope will always be in proportion to the view of God. The Godward gaze is the secret to hope. Consequently, Zechariah points the people to God—His power, His authority, His covenant faithfulness, and His Christ.

With this focus on hope, it is not surprising that Zechariah ranks as one of the most specifically and explicitly messianic books in the entire Old Testament. His messianic predictions detail aspects of Christ's person as the God-man and His work associated with each of His mediatorial functions as Prophet, Priest, and King. We will be looking at those key messianic texts in chapters 9–14, which consider the focus of hope, Christ in each of His mediatorial functions, for without Christ there is no hope at all. But overall the best way to sum up Zechariah's message of hope is this: *God's purpose for His people is even greater than their expectations.* In the light of that hope, Zechariah's ministry objective was to encourage God's people to live in victory and to serve with diligence in the certainty of God's purposed and promised blessing.

The Method

Zechariah 1:1 says directly that the word of the Lord came to Zechariah. As one of the "holy men of God," Zechariah spoke as he was "moved by the Holy Ghost" (2 Peter 1:21). His being inspired by God is indisputable since what he wrote is Scripture, all of which is God-breathed (2 Tim. 3:16). That God spoke to and through all the inspired prophets, including Zechariah, is fact; the mechanics of how God revealed His word, however, are not always well defined. Hebrews 1:1 informs that God spoke by the prophets at different times and in different ways. One of the ways God revealed His word was through visions. Very simply, in visions the Lord showed the prophet something that equated to His word. That prophets are sometimes called "seers" may relate to this particular mode of divine communication.

The designation "seer" would well describe Zechariah. After his initial declaration of the Lord's word (1:1–6), Zechariah records a series of eight visions that came to him as the word of the Lord, seemingly one after the other in a single night (1:7–6:8). In many ways Zechariah provides a casebook study of the nature of divinely revealed visions. Zechariah illustrates several salient points about visions. First, visions were personal and internal. What the prophet saw was not a drama open to public admission. Had others been standing next to Zechariah when he received the visions, they would not have seen what he saw. The vision was in his head; he was not making it up, but it was something taking place internally. Most likely, it would have appeared to anyone seeing Zechariah when he was seeing the Lord's word that he was in some sort of trance. Second, the recipient of the vision was usually an active participant in what he was seeing. Throughout the series of visions, Zechariah was conversing with an angel who interpreted what he saw and asked him some probing questions. This fact contrasts with dreams, another mode of divine revelation, where the recipient was completely passive and inactive. Significantly, the spiritual status of the recipients of dreams was irrelevant (for example, Pharaoh in Genesis 41 and Nebuchadnezzar in Daniel 2), whereas those receiving visions always had some degree of spiritual perception (for example, Abraham in Genesis 15 and Daniel in Daniel 7). Third, visions were highly symbolic, as evident from Daniel's odd-looking beasts (Dan. 7:1–7) and Zechariah's colored horses, flying rolls, and ephah basket stuffed with a woman. The key point is that visions were of divine origin and just as authoritative as any other mode of divine communication and revelation. Interpreting them can be a bit complicated, but they are the words of God nonetheless.

Another feature of note in Zechariah's method is the apocalyptic tone. This refers to a special genre of predictive prophecy that addresses the distant future, indeed the final consummation of God's plan and purpose. It is designed to give special assurances to God's people in dark and distressing days that God's redemptive purpose is unfailing and universal. Hence, every opposition to God's kingdom is doomed, and the kingdom of Christ will prevail: "And the LORD shall be king over all the earth: in that day shall there be one LORD, and his name one" (Zech. 14:9). Seeing the triumphant end puts all the problems of the present in perspective. Because the end has not yet come, it is as good for us as it was for those in Zechariah's day to look to that glorious future. Zechariah's message goes far beyond the concerns of just postexilic Israel; it assures the church today that God is in control and that everything is on course to accomplish His eternal purpose. Therefore, in reading and studying Zechariah, let us be encouraged to live in victory and to serve with diligence with a view to the certain blessing God has purposed and promised.

As we begin our survey of Zechariah, you may find the following outline helpful. It sums up the progression of Zechariah's prophecy.

I.   The Call to Repent (1:1–6)
II. The Visions to Encourage (1:7–6:15)
     A. Horses and the Myrtle Tree (1:8–17)
     B. Four Horns (1:18–21)
     C. Man with the Measuring Line (2:1–13)
     D. Joshua and the Branch (3:1–10)
     E. The Candlestick and Olive Trees (4:1–14)

Before we begin our survey, I should say something about my methodology. The length of the book precludes the kind of section-by-section synopsis that I followed for Haggai. It is not my purpose to write a commentary. My concern is to provide an overview of Zechariah's theme of hope by synthesizing data from the book under three heads: the foundation of hope, the focus of hope, and the fulfillment of hope. In so doing we will consider some texts in detail, but not all. I trust that this thematic overview will demonstrate what the book is about, whet the appetite for further study, and warm the heart with assurances from the Lord Himself for our dark days.

QUESTIONS

1. Summarize why Zechariah can be identified as an idealist.

2. How does hope relate to faith?

3. Why do we divide Zechariah's message into four main sections?

4. How does a dream differ from a vision?

5. How should Zechariah's message of hope affect Christian life today?

9

The Foundation of Hope

Without a sure foundation, hope is nothing more than wishful thinking. But nothing is surer than hope fixed on God and His word. The certainty of hope is not determined by how much or how fervently we believe, but rather by what we believe. The object of faith and hope is what determines their value and legitimacy. Hope goes way beyond any notion of positive thinking since it has no power, even though there is a common misconception that thinking positively can reverse whatever bad circumstance may be. Faith, and hope as its future expression, are not make-believe. We cannot believe truth or reality into existence, nor can truth or reality be denied out of existence. God, His word, and His purpose are absolutely independent of man's notions—either in terms of affirmation or abjuration. Hope is resting and ideally relaxing in the certainty of God and His word, a firm foundation indeed.

Zechariah proffers the message of hope by reiterating two principal evidences upon which to rest: God's promise and God's power. The promise is the basis of hope, and the power is its guarantee.

God's Promise

Because of the grandiose magnitude of his hope-filled message, Zechariah is careful to attribute what he says to God. He does not employ psychological gimmicks, emotional pleas, or any other tactic of personal persuasion to trick the people into being rededicated to the work on the temple. In exercising his prophetic commission, he simply repeats what God revealed to him. The fact of God's revelation is a primary interest, and well it should be, because if God were silent, hope would be impossible.

Zechariah begins his prophecy with the assurance that "the word of the LORD" came to him (1:1). Throughout the prophecy, he reinforces his message with that refrain. Take your Bible and trace the references for yourself (1:1, 7; 4:8; 6:9; 7:1, 4, 8; 8:1, 18; 9:1; and 12:1). In addition to the references to "the word of the LORD," Zechariah also refers to the fact of God's actual speaking (1:3, 4, 14, 16, 17; 2:5, 8, 10; 3:7, 10; 6:12; 7:9; 8:2, 3, 4, 6, 7, 9, 11, 14, 19, 20, 23; 11:4; 12:1, 4; 13:2, 8). If I have done my arithmetic correctly, that is about once in every five and one-half verses that Zechariah claims that what he is saying is actually what God is saying. I can't explain the supernatural mechanics of divine inspiration, but it seems to be remarkably clear that Zechariah was conscious that his words were "God-breathed" (2 Tim. 3:16) as he was being carried along by the Holy Spirit (2 Peter 1:21). The frequency of these assertions not only underscores the fact of divine revelation but also serves to give certainty and authority to the message. In essence, Zechariah assured his congregation that he was not making up the promises, which indeed would be too good to be true if coming from any other than God Himself.

This is the very notion expressed in Zechariah 8:6. After describing a scene of incredible blessing involving Jerusalem's restoration and reversal of its current circumstance, the Lord posed the question, "If it be marvellous in the eyes of the remnant of this people in these days, should it also be marvellous in mine eyes?" The word translated "marvelous" has the idea of being wonderful, extraordinary, beyond one's power or ability to do. It is a word often associated with God's extraordinary supernatural works, His miraculous acts. The point is that which is too difficult, indeed impossible, for man is not so for the Lord. If these promises were just Zechariah's fancies, they would be too good to be true. But they were true because they were God's words. Nothing is too hard for the Lord; rather, nothing is hard for Him at all.

Although there were several specific promises laid out before the people that we will consider later, there is one overarching divine word that subsumes all the rest: "Thus saith the LORD of hosts; I am jealous for Jerusalem and for Zion with a great jealousy.... Therefore thus saith the LORD; I am returned to Jerusalem with mercies" (1:14, 16). Again the prophet quoted the Lord as saying, "I was jealous for Zion with great jealousy.... Thus saith the LORD; I am returned unto Zion, and will dwell in the midst of Jerusalem" (8:2–3). These statements suggest two key thoughts, one about God's character and one about His actions. The jealousy of God (something about His character) generates divine intervention for His people (something about His actions).

That God is jealous begs for explanation since we normally regard jealousy as a vice and not a virtue. *Jealousy* is usually defined in terms of envy or covetousness and is often described as the green-eyed monster, as Shakespeare put it in his great tragedy of jealousy, *Othello*. It goes without saying, however, that there must be something pure and noble and virtuous about this word or it could not be attributed to the Lord. It is a perfection of God that demands total allegiance, for He will not share His glory with any other: "For thou shalt worship no other god: for the LORD, whose name is Jealous, is a jealous God" (Ex. 34:14). God's jealousy is a disposition of fervent zeal that manifests itself in the appropriate actions regarding the object of the zeal. Significantly, God directs His zeal to His own name, His own glory, His own word, and His own people. So infinitely concerned is God for these objects of His jealousy that He fervently guards them with His burning zeal, protecting them from any violation. To offend what He is jealous for earns His just retribution (Ex. 20:5); to honor what He is jealous for is to receive His favor (Ex. 20:6).

The Lord's language in declaring His jealousy for Jerusalem and Zion, His people (1:14; 8:2), intensifies the thought. In Hebrew, combining the verb with a noun of the same root (its cognate) is a way of expressing a superlative. In addition to the intensifying syntax, the adjective "great" modifies jealousy. The point was unmistakably clear and profoundly remarkable. The statement "I am jealous...with a great jealousy" could well be translated "I am really and intensely zealous." That intense and fervent zeal had to find expression; the attitude of zeal is accompanied by appropriate action.

The appropriate action constituted the overarching promise God was making for His people, the object of His jealousy. The promised action was that God would return to Jerusalem with mercies (1:16) and would dwell with His people (8:3). The word "mercies" is an anthropopathism (a figure of speech by which human emotions or feelings are attributed to God) to help us comprehend something of His otherwise incomprehensible nature. The root's literal significance designates the womb and by extension refers to the compassion or pity a mother would feel as she would see her child in some distress and then do whatever she had to do to alleviate that distress. But fathers are capable of this kind of pity as well (see Ps. 103:13). "Mercies," the plural form, may refer to multiple acts of mercy, but more likely it is an abstract plural used to intensify the idea of the noun "great mercy." Hebrew often uses the grammatical plural for reasons other than enumerating countables. The essence of the promise would be then that God, seeing the afflictions and troubles of His people, would be moved in compassion to intervene in their behalf to alleviate the trouble. God's dwelling with His people denoted His presence and fellowship with them. During the years of captivity, the Lord had withdrawn His presence and the experience of His fellowship (see Hos. 5:15), but things were going to change. There was reason to hope because God saw their estate and nothing could hinder or frustrate His fervent zeal to make everything right. The promise, in the broadest of terms, was that everything was going to be good even though every circumstance around them seemed to be bad. They had God's word on it.

God's Power

Talk is cheap. In the heat of passion or in zeal for a cause, men may say things that in reality they have no ability to perform. But that is not the case with God; His promises are not empty words. If God's promise is the basis of hope, then God's power is the guarantee that hope is not just a wish that maybe will come true. Hope in God's promise is reasonable because His word is reality. Behind God's fervent zeal and hot jealousy for His word and His people are infinite power and absolute authority.

Zechariah highlights this infinite power and absolute authority in multiple ways. Most outstanding is the title he habitually uses when referring to the Lord. It is imperative to remember that the names or titles of God used in the Scripture are never selected haphazardly. The names of God are one of the means of divine self-revelation and communicate some truth about God that is appropriate to the context in which it occurs. It is a key part of the interpretive procedure to factor that meaning into the understanding of any given passage. This is true for both Testaments, but particularly in the Old Testament, which employs significantly more specific and different titles than the New.

Unquestionably, the most common title for God in Zechariah is the "LORD of hosts." It occurs over fifty times throughout the prophecy, approximately in one out of every four verses. It is virtually impossible to read the prophecy without taking note of this title, and taking note is precisely what Zechariah intended his audience, then and now, to do.

This title especially declares God's power and authority. The word "hosts" is the Hebrew word for "armies," suggesting a military orientation. It designates the Lord as the commander in chief who has the authority to order all those under His command to do His bidding. The expression occurs throughout the Old Testament, but is particularly frequent in the postexilic period, as reflected in Zechariah's prophecy. In different contexts and at different times those enlisted in the army varied. For instance, Deuteronomy 4:19 uses the word "host" to refer to the celestial bodies: "the sun, and the moon, and the stars, even all the host of heaven." Psalm 103:20–21 indicates that the angels constitute the Lord's army: "Bless the LORD, ye his angels.... Bless ye the LORD, all ye his hosts; ye ministers of his, that do his pleasure." When David challenged Goliath, he did so in "the name of the LORD of hosts, the God of the armies of Israel" (1 Sam. 17:45). So sometimes it appeared that Israel itself constituted the army (see also Josh. 5:14–15). It is my opinion that in Zechariah the "armies" refer to the totality of God's creation that He has at His disposal to order and accomplish His word and purpose.

Now factor that into the message. Zechariah put before the people the prospect of blessings that were marvelous, extraordinary, and grandiose—all beyond human comprehension. But they were not in doubt in the least because ordering every blessing was the Commander in Chief whose authority was supreme and whose army was invincible. Nothing could hinder the promise because nothing could resist God's power.

That the LORD, or Jehovah, is part of this compound title is amazingly significant, as well as the fact that it occurs frequently alone throughout Zechariah. Jehovah is the covenant name of God that is especially linked to His saving and redemptive work in behalf of His people. It declares His absolute existence, independence, and sovereignty, but primarily is linked to His covenant revelation and commitments to His people. The God who has all the power of creation at His disposal is the personal God who has guaranteed by covenant to act in behalf of His people. With Jehovah of Armies behind every promise, there was every reason to hope.

Zechariah developed the thought of God's power and authority in other ways than just through the divine title "Jehovah of Hosts" that he associated so closely with God's promise. Every evidence of divine power reinforced the certainty of hope's foundation. For instance, in 12:1 the prophet identifies the Lord as the Creator (see also 10:1), the One "which stretcheth forth the heavens, and layeth the foundation of the earth, and formeth the spirit of man within him." Throughout Scripture, creation theology testifies to the unique power and authority of God. Only God can create; God owns what He creates; and He has the sovereign right, therefore, to govern what He owns in whatever way He desires. So it is not surprising to see how Zechariah demonstrates God's sovereign control over all the affairs of the world. At the beginning of his message, he indicated that the Lord was the active cause in

Judah's recent captivity. He explicitly expressed this when he said, "Like as the LORD of hosts thought to do unto us...so hath he dealt with us" (1:6; see also 8:14–15). The word "thought" has the idea of "to purpose" or "to devise" and thus refers to God's irresistible plan. Not only does the Lord exercise His sovereignty over Israel but also over the pagan nations. Zechariah 1:15 suggests that even though God used the nations as the instrument for afflicting His people, he would hold them accountable for their actions. The primary theme in chapters 9–11 is God's activity in overthrowing the pagan nations that are ignorant of Him, but nonetheless accountable to Him and responsible before Him. This is a common thread in the opening visions as well, and we will look at that in due course when we think about the fulfillment of hope.

My point for now is simply to establish that Zechariah's message of hope was well founded. Given that God was the source of the message and the power behind the message, hoping in the message was most sensible. It is never a vain or futile thing to hope in the Lord. The affirmation and prayer of the psalmist are a good way to sum up what I want us to learn from this chapter. Here is the affirmation: "I hope in thy word" (Ps. 119:81). Here is the prayer: "Remember the word unto thy servant, upon which thou hast caused me to hope" (Ps. 119:49). It gets better when we consider the specifics of what God has promised. That is next in our study.

QUESTIONS

1. Why is the object of faith (what we believe) so important?

2. What evidence is there that Zechariah knew he was ministering (preaching and writing) under the inspiration of the Holy Spirit?

3. Can you think of other instances in the Old Testament when the Lord declared that nothing was too hard or difficult for Him? (Hint: Look up *hard* or *difficult* in a concordance.)

4. In what sense is jealousy good?

5. What evidences or proofs does Zechariah give of God's power?

6. Why is the title "Lord of Hosts" so important in Zechariah? What implications of that title are important in your life?

10

The Focus of Hope:
The Prophet

In speaking to a group of antagonists, the Lord Jesus instructed, "Search the scriptures; for in them ye think ye have eternal life: and they are they which testify of me" (John 5:39). In the same context to the same crowd He said, "Had ye believed Moses, ye would have believed me: for he wrote of me" (John 5:46). What Christ said about Moses is equally true about Zechariah. Indeed, according to what the risen Jesus said to the forlorn disciples on the Emmaus road, that assessment applies to the entire Old Testament. He started with Moses and progressed through the prophets as "he expounded unto them in all the scriptures the things concerning himself" (Luke 24:27; also Luke 24:44 where He specifically adds a reference to the Psalms). Peter later reaffirmed that hermeneutic key to the Bible when he said that the Spirit of Christ was in the Old Testament prophets, so that what they wrote "testified beforehand the sufferings of Christ, and the glory that should follow" (1 Peter 1:11). So as we read and study Zechariah, we must do so on "Christ alert." To miss his message of Messiah is to miss the focus, the principal component in his message of hope. It was as true in his day as it was in Paul's and as remains true in our day: to be without Christ is to be without hope (Eph. 2:12).

In many ways, Zechariah ranks as one of the most specific and explicit of messianic prophecies in all the Old Testament. It would not at all be a stretch to designate this prophecy as "The Gospel according to Zechariah." As he directs attention to the coming Christ, most remarkable is his focus on the mediatorial functions of Christ as the ideal Prophet, Priest, and King. Focusing on God's redemptive purpose to reverse the curse in and through Christ was key to fostering and rekindling hope in a people who in so many ways had given up hope in the face of the discouragements of the day. To see Christ was and is to see the heart of God's promise and to be assured of every other word, for all the promises of God are yea and amen in Christ (2 Cor. 1:20).

The Westminster Shorter Catechism succinctly defines how Christ carries out the prophetic office: "Christ executeth the office of a prophet, in revealing to us, by his Word and Spirit, the will of God for our salvation" (Q. 24). Speaking of the Lord Jesus in prophetic terms, Hebrews declares that God spoke in various ways through the prophets but has now revealed His final word to man by His Son, "whom he hath appointed heir of all things" (1:1–2). That sums up the message of hope, for without that ultimate Word, salvation would be impossible.

Put simply, a prophet is God's representative to man, one who speaks with divine authority to men in God's behalf. Who better than the very Son of God, Himself God, could represent God to man? Christ, indeed, is the ideal Prophet because Christ is God. Although all the Old

Testament prophets were men of God speaking for God, how imperfectly they represented God when compared to the Lord Jesus, who was "the brightness of his glory, and the express image of his person" (Heb. 1:3). Similarly, Paul also said of Christ that He is "the image of the invisible God" and that "in him dwelleth all the fulness of the Godhead bodily" (Col. 1:15; 2:9). Although Hebrews and Colossians use two different words for "image," the sense of both is essentially the same. That Christ is the image of God does not mean that He is a mere reflection or representation of God; rather, it affirms that He is the very manifestation of God. In the person of Jesus Christ, invisible deity assumed visibility. A key component to Christ's being *the* Prophet is His true and absolute deity.

The New Testament makes this truth explicitly clear, and so does Zechariah. Admittedly, Zechariah fuses into any given context aspects of the work of Christ that from a systematic theological perspective would constitute different categories. But this is to be expected and is not unique to Zechariah since the Bible is not written according to a theological outline of separate doctrines. At this point I want to look at a couple of texts that, among other truths, explicitly declare the deity of the Messiah, the essential requirement of His ideal mediatorial "prophethood."

Zechariah 13:7 marks a transition from the deception of false prophets to the person and work of the true Prophet. It is an important text because of both its identification of the Messiah and its statement of His sacrificial death: "Awake, O sword, against my shepherd, and against the man that is my fellow, saith the LORD of hosts: smite the shepherd, and the sheep shall be scattered." Christ's words fix the application of this verse to the events of the crucifixion (Matt. 26:31). In particular, this verse makes two great statements that highlight the deity of Messiah. Hope is based on who He is and on what He does.

However, before I address those statements, I should comment on why the transition in Zechariah 13 from false to true occurs at verse 7 and not at verse 6, notwithstanding a widely found interpretation that views verse 6 as messianic: "And one shall say unto him, What are these wounds in thine hands? Then he shall answer, Those with which I was wounded in the house of my friends." It is a hermeneutical error to miss seeing Christ where He is in the Old Testament text; it is also an error to see Him where He is not. Unquestionably, the reference to the wounds in the hands that were inflicted in the house of friends is redolent of Christ's being nailed to the cross at the relentless urging of His own people, for "He came unto his own, and his own received him not" (John 1:11). But surface similarity is not the primary factor in the interpretive process and certainly cannot override the context. In context, the question "What are these wounds in thine hands?" is directed to a false prophet who, along with his counterparts, had fallen into disfavor and was under the threat of the death sentence if and when caught (13:2–3). Even though they tried to disguise themselves (13:4–5), one of them had something exposed, the wounds in the hands, that raised suspicion, potentially giving him away as a false prophet. The Hebrew text refers literally to wounds "between the hands," not in the hands. This is an idiom referring to the back or chest area, that body surface often the target of self-mutilation as a pagan means of invoking deity (see 1 Kings 18:28 where the prophets of Baal mutilated themselves). So it is not likely that the words of a false prophet, bearing the marks of his trade, are prophetic of the nail prints in the hands of Jesus.

Although not in verse 6, Christ is wonderfully and unmistakably the focus of verse 7. What makes verse 7 such a remarkable statement is that the speaker is the Lord of Hosts. The Lord first addresses the Messiah as "my shepherd." Understanding the significance of this requires factoring in some antecedent revelation. In other words, Zechariah did not introduce the messianic import of the title, but rather builds on a previously established theology. The previous revelation informs us how to interpret what Zechariah's later revelation means. The messianic significance of this title occurs as early as Genesis 49:24. The "shepherd, the stone of Israel" would come from the mighty God of Jacob. The use of the title "shepherd" was common in the ancient world. Based on the obvious pastoral imagery, the appellative was frequently employed even by pagan kings to designate their authoritative rule. The title refers to sovereign kingship and thus points to Christ's being the mediatorial King. But there is an aspect of the shepherd theology that avers the deity of the ideal Shepherd, which is why I'm suggesting it communicates something about His being the ideal Prophet as well.

I'm going to set Zechariah aside briefly to establish the foundation for the remarkable statement in 13:7. Follow the progression in Ezekiel 34 to see the point. That chapter begins with God's condemnation of bad shepherds who feed themselves rather than the sheep and leave the sheep to wander aimlessly. The Lord then announced that He would perform the shepherd's duty by seeking the lost and sick sheep (vv. 12, 16), bringing them safely and securely into the fold. When He found them, He would graciously meet their needs. He would bind the broken and strengthen the sick (v. 16); this pictures forgiveness. He would feed the hungry (v. 14); this pictures provision. He would give rest (v. 15); this pictures peace and security. Having identified Himself as the Good Shepherd, the Lord then declared that He would raise up a shepherd to save His people: "And I will set up one shepherd over them, and he shall feed them, even my servant David; he shall feed them, and he shall be their shepherd. And I the LORD will be their God, and my servant David a prince among them; I the Lord have spoken it" (Ezek. 34:23–24).

Ezekiel refers to David in the ideal sense of the greater-than-David who is the ultimate fulfillment of the Davidic covenant. Jeremiah and Hosea illustrate that "David" is itself a messianic title. Both prophets connect the title "David" to the Lord. Jeremiah says the time will come when the people will "serve the LORD their God, and David their king, whom I will raise up unto them" (Jer. 30:9). Hosea similarly says, "Afterward shall the children of Israel return, and seek the LORD their God, and David their king" (Hos. 3:5). In both texts the "and" should be interpreted and could be translated as an explicative (that which explains) rather than a copulative (that which connects): "the LORD their God, even David their king."

So in Ezekiel, the shepherd is the Lord, yet the shepherd is distinct from the Lord. He is the perfect manifestation of God—hence, the perfect Prophet. This dual identification points to that mysterious trinitarian relationship between God the Father and God the Son. Zechariah's brief statement "my shepherd" must be understood in the light of Ezekiel's theology. The pronoun "my" suggests both the divine appointment and the special relationship that exists between the shepherd and Jehovah. It parallels precisely the Lord's declaration in Psalm 2:6: "Yet have I set my king upon my holy hill of Zion." The Lord's referring to the Messiah as "my shepherd" ("my king") is a subtle statement, but one that is loaded with theological significance.

But Zechariah goes further in expressing the deity of the Messiah when he records that the Lord of Hosts identifies His shepherd as "the man that is my fellow" (13:7). Both antecedent revelation and the lexemes (vocabulary units) are significant. The word "man" often designates man in his strength, referring to a hero figure. The word comes from the same root that Isaiah uses in 9:6, the classic messianic text that lists a series of titles that describe the character of Immanuel. Isaiah identified the Son to be born as the mighty God. This literally says "God, the defender/guardian." The term "God" (*El*) applies only to deity and designates God in His power and transcendent majesty. The term "defender/guardian," the root occurring in Zechariah 13:7, is not uniquely a divine word, but the Scripture does apply it to the Lord, identifying Him as the security of His people. Isaiah uses the same expression in referring directly to Jehovah, the Holy One of Israel (Isa. 10:20–21).

Years later, but still antecedent to Zechariah, Jeremiah used the expression as he addressed the Lord in prayer: "the Great, the Mighty God, the LORD of hosts, is his name" (Jer. 32:18). Many years earlier, Moses declared, "For the LORD your God is God of gods, and Lord of lords, a great God, a mighty" (Deut. 10:17). That this title became part of messianic vocabulary and theology is clear from Psalm 45, an unmistakably messianic psalm. Verse 3 entreats the Messiah, "Gird thy sword upon thy thigh, O most mighty." So by the time Zechariah uses this term "man" (the mighty one) to refer to the Lord's shepherd, it was well charged with messianic import pointing to the Messiah's deity.

Also of consequence is the word "fellow." This word occurs only here and in Leviticus. Usually translated "neighbor" in Leviticus, it refers to those who have things in common, such as laws and privileges. It would be inappropriate for God in the Zechariah context to apply this term to mere mortal man. This one, God's associate or nearest one, stands not merely in proximity to God but is equal with God. He participates and shares in the divine nature; He is God. So the Lord's referring to His shepherd as His fellow conforms to trinitarian theology that Christ and the Father are distinct in person, yet one in essence.

Zechariah hints elsewhere that he understood this unique relationship. In 11:4–14 the rejected shepherd (against whom the sword is summoned in 13:7) is Jehovah. In 12:10 Jehovah says, "They shall look upon *me* whom they have pierced, and they shall mourn for *him*" (italics added). The shift in pronouns from the first to the third person testifies to the distinctive association.

That God would send His perfect representative, His Son, was the great message of hope. I would not be at all surprised if Zechariah 13:7 was in Christ's mind when in the New Testament chapter on the Good Shepherd he declared, "I and my Father are one" (John 10:30). Christ Jesus is the ideal Prophet because He is God. I can't say that too often, and we cannot believe it too much.

The Lord Jesus qualifies as the ideal Prophet not only by virtue of who He is but also by what He does. The function of the prophet is to reveal, "by his Word and Spirit, the will of God for our salvation" (Westminster Shorter Catechism, Q. 24). Christ's execution of this function is unique and distinct from every lesser prophet since He Himself is the way of salvation that He reveals and declares (John 14:6). Consequently, it is not unexpected to see united into a single context facets of each part of Christ's mediatorial work.

This certainly is the case in Zechariah 13:7. I have focused particularly on the prophetic component in terms of what is revealed concerning Christ's divine nature. But His designation as shepherd speaks directly to His kingship since this is a common title for sovereigns. The text is also important because of its statement of the Messiah's sacrificial death, which points directly to His mediatorial priesthood. Interestingly, this is not the only passage Jesus links directly to the events of His crucifixion (Matt. 26:31); He marks another parallel to Zechariah's prophecy when He says, "I am the good shepherd: the good shepherd giveth his life for the sheep" (John 10:11).

God's way of salvation required the sacrifice of the shepherd, "the fellow" of God. Zechariah 13:7 squelches any notion that the Messiah's death was anything other than the eternal purpose of God. The verse begins with Jehovah of Hosts commanding the sword to awaken and smite His shepherd. That God demanded the death of His equal (fellow) speaks volumes concerning the seriousness of sin and the immutability of divine justice. In Pauline language, it is only by and because of the death of Christ that God is both just and justifier (Rom. 3:26). In Zechariah's terms, it is only because God bade the sword awake against His shepherd that a cleansing fountain could be opened "for sin and for uncleanness" (13:1).

QUESTIONS

1. Given the definition of the prophetic office, why can it be said that Christ is the ideal Prophet?

2. How does the ministry (work) of Christ differ from every other prophet?

3. Notwithstanding the surface similarity, why is the question, "What are these wounds in thine hands?" not directed to Christ?

4. In what sense can it be said that Christ is David?

5. Summarize the trinitarian evidence from Zechariah 13:7.

6. What are the implications of Christ's being killed by divine command?

11

The Focus of Hope:
The Priest

Christ also executes His mediatorial office by functioning as a priest; He is the ideal Priest to whom every other lesser priest in the Levitical order pointed. The Westminster Shorter Catechism cogently describes how Christ carries out the priestly office: "Christ executeth the office of a priest, in his once offering up of himself a sacrifice to satisfy divine justice and reconcile us to God, and in making continual intercession for us" (Q. 25). In simple terms, a priest is man's representative before God. It is obvious from the Catechism's statement that the priesthood of Christ brings us to the heart of His mission and the ultimate purpose of His incarnation. Christ came to save His people, and saving His people required the shedding of His blood in sacrifice. As the deity of Christ is essential to His being the perfect Prophet, the humanity of Christ is essential to His being the perfect Priest. The only hope for sinners is that "God was manifest in the flesh" (1 Tim. 3:16).

Zechariah's message of hope, then, necessarily focuses attention on the priestly work of Christ. His initial vision of the man on the red horse, who is identified as the Angel of the Lord (a preincarnate messianic manifestation), highlights something of Christ's intercessory ministry, a priestly operation. Having received the report that "all the earth sitteth still, and is at rest" (1:11), the Angel intercedes in behalf of Jerusalem, that the Lord might turn away from His indignation and have mercy (1:12). His prayer was ground for hope because the Lord answered Him "with good words and comfortable words" (1:13) and gave the assurance that He would return "to Jerusalem with mercies" (1:16). Here is Old Testament evidence from the preincarnate Christ that illustrates the testimony of the incarnate Christ when He said that He knew the Father always heard Him when He prayed (John 11:41). That remains an encouraging hope for every believer—to know that He ever lives to make intercession (Heb. 7:25).

We have already seen something of Messiah's sacrificial death in terms of the Lord's commanding the sword to awake against the shepherd (13:7) and the reference to the day when the nation would look on the Lord whom they had pierced (12:10). At this point, I want to consider two outstanding passages that focus on the humanity of Christ, which is so crucial to His functioning as the mediatorial Priest. Both passages refer to Messiah as the Branch (3:8; 6:12), a title that by Zechariah's time was already loaded with messianic significance.

As is so often the case in studying the Bible, it is important to factor in previous revelation to the particular point of study. This is a critical component in interpreting in context. Therefore, understanding the context of Zechariah's references to the Branch requires defining the term and reflecting on its antecedent use as a messianic title by Isaiah and Jeremiah.

At first glance this theologically full title of Messiah does not appear to be a particularly flattering expression. The common noun is based on a root verb that means "to sprout or bud." It refers to a new shoot that buds on a stump or in unexpected and unwanted places. Although Ezekiel does not use the word with messianic significance, he illustrates the basic sense of the word in his allegory of the two eagles and the transplanted cedar branches in chapter 17. The verb form occurs at the beginning of verse 6. Not long after the cut-off branch was planted, it sprouted, showing signs of new life. The noun form occurs in the middle of verse 9, where the Lord asks whether the leaves on this new sprout will wither. There was a sign of new life, but it was so fragile that survival seemed unlikely. The point is that the term does not refer to a large, strong bough that extends majestically from a well-rooted tree; it refers to something that is tender and fragile, yet full of promising life in an unlikely place.

This imagery underscores the messianic application in two ways. First, that the Messiah is a branch vividly pictures His humiliation. The Messiah did not appear with all the pomp, circumstance, and manifest glory that He deserved and inherently and eternally was His. On the contrary, He humbled Himself, becoming a man and becoming obedient as a humble servant unto the death of the cross (Phil. 2:6–8). There was nothing about Christ that to natural sight would identify Him as the eternal Son of God; He appeared as an ordinary man. What condescension it was for God to become manifest in flesh!

Second, that the Messiah is a branch vividly testifies to God's faithful fulfilling of the covenant promise. This title has a special link to the Seed promise that reached its Old Testament climax in the covenant promise to David that his seed, or descendant, would sit forever on the throne, ruling a universal and everlasting kingdom (2 Samuel 7). King after king sat on David's throne, each one disqualified as the ultimate and unconditional fulfillment of the promise. When the ultimate Seed finally came in the fullness of time, there was no king at all from David's family, and there had not been for hundreds of years. From every natural perspective, it appeared that David's dynasty was defunct. But from the stump of David's fallen kingdom, there appeared a new green shoot of life. There was life in the promise; the ideal King had arrived. The title "Branch" discloses the real humanity of Messiah by linking His lineage to David's.

Although each of the messianic passages using this title makes a unique contribution, all declare the humble humanity of Christ as the fulfillment of the covenant promise. Isaiah's special focus is that the Branch who is man is also God: "In that day shall the branch of the LORD be beautiful and glorious" (Isa. 4:2). This should be interpreted "the Branch who is Jehovah." Isaiah's expression declares the Messiah to be the God-man. Jeremiah's special focus is on the kingly operation of the Branch, who actively behaves according to the demands of God, accomplishing everything God has promised and purposed in the Davidic covenant (Jer. 23:5; 33:15). According to Isaiah, the Branch (the God-man) is the ideal Prophet, who manifests God to men. According to Jeremiah, the "righteous Branch" is the ideal King, whose name is "THE LORD OUR RIGHTEOUSNESS" (*Jehovah Tsidkenu*, as in Robert M. M'Cheyne's well-known hymn) and whose reign is prosperous and just (Jer. 23:5–6). It is not surprising, then, that Zechariah advances Branch theology by identifying the Branch as the ideal Priest. It is a fitting way for Zechariah, the prophet of hope, to refer to Messiah. In the midst of so much hopelessness, the prophet points to the new shoot of life. In the Branch, there is hope after all.

Zechariah 3:8 identifies the Branch as the servant of the Lord, which only adds to the messianic import of this focal point of hope. The designation "servant of the Lord" is an honorific title expressing both a special relationship between the servant and the Lord and a functionary subordination in which the servant performs obediently the will of the Lord. Throughout the Old Testament, specially called and used men of God were designated God's servants. Moses, more than any other saint (about forty times), was called the servant of the Lord (e.g., Deut. 34:5; Josh. 1:1–2). But several others enjoyed the honor of that designation: Abraham (Gen. 26:24), Caleb (Num. 14:24), Joshua (Josh. 24:29), Samson (Judg. 15:18), David (2 Sam. 7:19–20), Elijah (1 Kings 18:36), Job (Job 1:8), Nehemiah (Neh. 1:6, 10), prophets and priests generally (Ps. 134:1; Jer. 7:25), and even the nation of Israel as a whole (Jer. 30:10; 46:27–28). Sometimes even the unexpected received the title: Nebuchadnezzar, the pagan Babylonian king, unknowingly was raised up and used by God to accomplish the Lord's will (Jer. 27:6; 43:10). What unites this list is that the servant was one God especially chose to stand at the head of a people to perform a special mission for Him in behalf of the people. It was a position of great honor and grave responsibility. It is a fitting messianic title since Christ stands in a unique relationship to the Lord and performs the divine will to absolute perfection.

It was Isaiah who, under divine inspiration, began to make the connection between the servant and the promised Messiah. Referring to the servant theme more than thirty times in his prophecy, Isaiah points to the failures of lesser servants to establish the need for the ideal Servant who faithfully and obediently does whatever is necessary to accomplish God's purpose of saving His people. Significantly, Isaiah 52:13–53:12, the climax of Isaiah's servant songs, points ahead with historical precision to Christ's sacrifice, His priestly work. All this makes the point that Zechariah's identification of the Branch as the Lord's servant advances what Isaiah started and must be understood in the light of that previous revelation. Zechariah did not write in a theological vacuum, and we cannot read his prophecy in one either.

Zechariah's naming of the Branch as servant occurs in the fourth of his series of eight visions that give an overview of God's plan for fulfilling the promised hope. I'm going to reserve my exposition and synopsis of the vision for the next chapter except to say that Zechariah 3 is one of the most vivid pictures anywhere of God's gracious act in justifying sinners. If anything is clear in this vision, it is that justification is based on God's bringing forth His "servant the BRANCH," who will make it possible for God to "remove the iniquity of that land in one day" (3:8–9).

It is impossible to think about justification without thinking about what Christ has done. The prophecy of the Branch, God's servant, points to Christ in His humanity and the life of humble obedience whereby He earned merit before God, weaving for us that robe of righteousness. He was made of woman under the law. His removal of iniquity in a single day points to His cross, on which He shed His blood in atonement for our sins. Because of what Christ did in His life and in His death, we can be justified before the Holy God. The bottom line is that Zechariah 3 details facts about both Messiah's person (His humanity) and His work (His sacrifice) that are essential to His priesthood.

In Zechariah 6:9–15, the prophet again affirms the humanity of the Branch and links Him directly to the priesthood. The paragraph gives the details of an object lesson involving Joshua the high priest. The prophet is instructed to enact a coronation ceremony at which event a splendid crown (the plural in Hebrew expresses the idea of excellence) is placed on the head of Joshua. That symbolic gesture of a priest wearing a crown is accompanied with the declaration, "Behold the man whose name is The BRANCH; and he shall grow up [the verb is the same root word as branch] out of his place.... He shall bear the glory, and shall sit and rule upon his throne; and he shall be a priest upon his throne" (6:12–13). The particular focus of this object lesson is the uniting of the offices of priest and king in the person of the Branch. The significance of this is outstanding since the Lord had made an important dichotomy between these two mediatorial offices. Hermeneutically, it is an inviolable messianic clue that whenever these two offices are united in a single person, the reference must be to Christ. The significance is obvious. Inherent in the term "Branch" is identification with the royal line of David. The identification of the Branch as man helps establish the priestly connection with Joshua, because a priest had to be one of those he represented. Humanity is an essential qualification for priesthood. After the symbolic coronation, the crown was removed from Joshua and kept "for a memorial in the temple of the LORD" (6:14). Joshua was part of a wonderful picture, but he was not the reality. In fact, this object lesson confirmed the obsolescence of the Levitical priesthood and fostered hope in a coming royal Priest who would be after the order of Melchizedek and not Aaron. Only Jesus, the Great High Priest to come, could wear and keep the crown.

QUESTIONS

1. Why is the humanity of Christ essential to His being a priest?

2. What happens in Zechariah's opening vision that points to Christ's priesthood?

3. What is the imagery suggested by the title "Branch"?

4. What are the key passages in the Old Testament that use this title? Sum up the teaching of each passage.

5. How should the messianic title "servant" be understood? Understanding Zechariah's use of the term depends on factoring in the message of which earlier prophet?

12

The Focus of Hope:
The King

The final component of Christ's mediatorial office is His kingship. Christ is the ideal King to whom every lesser king pointed. The failures of every other king intensified the desire and expectation for the perfect King to come. When Zechariah preached, David's throne was vacant, and there was no prospect of a king in sight. It appeared that hope was gone, and any hoping was in vain. But contrary to appearance, everything was working according to divine plan. Years earlier, Ezekiel had announced God's indictment of Davidic kingship: "Remove the diadem.... It shall be no more, until he come whose right it is; and I will give it him" (Ezek. 21:26–27; cf. with Gen. 49:10 ["Shiloh" means "to whom it belongs"]). The vacancy was God's plan, and so was the coming of the rightful heir to that covenant throne. Every moment the throne was without an occupant was a moment closer to Shiloh. A prevalent point in Zechariah's message was to focus hope in that King who was certain to come.

The Westminster Shorter Catechism concisely explains how Christ carries out the kingly office: "Christ executeth the office of a king, in subduing us to himself, in ruling and defending us, and in restraining and conquering all his and our enemies" (Q. 26). Ironically, the kingship of Christ is one of the most obvious of His messianic operations, yet in some ways the most confusing. As the Second Person of the Trinity, the Son of God is the absolute sovereign over all things. As God, He exercises dominion over His entire creation. There is, therefore, a kingship that the Savior has by virtue of His being God. On the other hand, as the Christ, the Son of God was anointed and commissioned with a kingship that is vitally connected to the mediatorial work of grace. The messianic kingship refers specifically to Christ's authority to rule for God's glory and for the ingathering of the whole number of God's elect. By this special kingship, the Lord Jesus procures, protects, and perfects the church. His rule is ultimately universal, irresistible, providential, and enduring until "the end, when he shall have delivered up the kingdom to God, even the Father" (1 Cor. 15:24).

Zechariah's message of hope as it relates to Christ's kingship can be summed up under three heads: His character, His coming, and His conquering. The throne was empty, but there was every reason to hope.

His Character

"Out of him came forth the corner, out of him the nail, out of him the battle bow, out of him every oppressor together" (Zech. 10:4). Admittedly, not all agree with my interpretation of this text, but I do believe that here Zechariah is delineating character traits of the messianic King. The person described in Zechariah 10:4 is God's answer to the bad shepherds (rulers) in verses 2–3 who had troubled the flock of His people. The Lord of Hosts would visit His people and reverse their fortunes. The agent by whom the bad shepherds would be punished and the flock blessed is by implication the Good Shepherd King described as the corner, the nail, the battle bow, and the absolute ruler. In the original Hebrew, the statement "from him" (from the Lord) precedes each of these four titles, suggesting the divine anointing and commission of the Messiah to conduct His ministry.

That Christ is the *corner* testifies to His being the sure and stable foundation. This same word occurs in Isaiah's more extensive description: "Behold, I lay in Zion for a foundation a stone, a tried stone, a precious *corner* stone, a sure foundation: he that believeth shall not make haste" (Isa. 28:16, italics added). Likewise, it is the word in Psalm 118:22: "The stone which the builders refused is become the head stone of the *corner*" (italics added). The New Testament demands the christological interpretation (see Matt. 21:42; Acts 4:11; 1 Peter 2:4–8). In contrast to the vain and worthless objects of trust mentioned in Zechariah 10:2 (idols, diviners, dreamers), from the Lord would come the corner, the only trustworthy object for faith. That was true then, and it is true now. The object of faith determines the value of faith, and the only object of saving faith is Christ.

That Christ is the *nail* testifies to His ability to bear the load in supporting His people. This nail is a peg in the wall for hanging items. Unless the peg is solid, it will be useless for hanging anything. Ezekiel plays on this thought when he says that the "wood" of a vine would be a worthless pin for hanging vessels (Ezek. 15:3). Isaiah's report of Eliakim's

promotion to administer the keys to David's house illustrates this function of the nail: "And I will fasten him as a
nail in a sure place.... And they shall hang upon him all
the glory [weight] of his father's house." Sadly, Eliakim's
nail loosened, and the burden hanging on it fell off (Isa.
22:23–25). This failure of what seemed to be a sure support
points to the fact that there is only one nail that is strong
enough and sure enough to hold any burden. That unfailing nail is Christ. In contrast to the bad shepherds, who
took advantage of and increased the burden of the people,
the Lord would fix an immovable nail that would hold up
under any weight and load. It is good to know that Christ
did not merely bear the load of our guilt and sin but that
He is ever able to bear the load of our troubles and cares.
We can hang it all on Him.

That Christ is the *battle bow* testifies to His being the
active champion and warrior for His people. This highlights
that aspect of His mediatorial kingship in which He subdues and conquers all of His and our enemies. The psalmist
speaks of the same activity in the great royal and messianic
Psalm 45: "Thine arrows are sharp in the heart of the king's
enemies; whereby the people fall under thee" (v. 5). This
kingly behavior is on the surface of the Zechariah text. It is
this divinely sent battle bow who will execute God's anger
against the bad shepherds and punish the goats. Certainly,
the final manifestation of this warrior King will come when
He rides in on that white horse with a sharp sword in His
mouth to smite the nations (Rev. 19:12–15). In the meantime, Christ is the able and unfailing defender of His people.

That Christ is the *absolute ruler* testifies to His certain sovereignty. The translation of this last line is notoriously difficult. The word the King James Version translates as "oppressor" is the word I am focusing on when I say that Christ is the absolute ruler. There is no question that the word designates a ruler, and many occurrences of the word in the Old Testament refer to hard taskmasters or slave drivers who would use whatever means they desired to force their subjects into compliance. This explains the translation "oppressor." However, I would suggest that the word itself simply defines one who has ultimate authority over another. The character of the ruler determines whether his rule is cruel and oppressive. The parallelism with the other three expressions demands that this title refer to the same person. Therefore, the ruler with absolute authority over His subjects is Christ. His rule is not oppressive, but it is absolute nonetheless. This is a most fitting designation of Christ in the immediate context. The people knew well the oppression of the bad shepherds (rulers). What a relief it would be to know the kind despotism of the Messiah King. Submitting to the absolute authority of Christ is always a relief; moreover, it is the wise thing to do. He will rule either by grace or by the rod of iron. The advice of Psalm 2:12 is appropriate in view of this absolute rule of Christ: "Kiss the Son, lest he be angry, and ye perish from the way, when his wrath is kindled but a little. Blessed are all they that put their trust in him." If He is the absolute ruler, it is best to be a citizen rather than an enemy of His kingdom. That was true then; it is true now.

His Coming

Zechariah 9:9 is one of the most famous messianic prophecies in this book that is so rich in messianic promise and theology. The prophet commands Zion to rejoice because the ideal King is coming. Both Zechariah and the New Testament place this coming during the time of Messiah's first advent. Zechariah sets the prophecy against the backdrop of a prophecy concerning Greece's world conquests and God's defeat of Greece. Significantly, it is in this prophetic revelation about Greece that Zechariah announces the coming King. The contribution that Greece made culturally and linguistically to the fullness of time has received much deserved attention. Although the details of those contributions are not enumerated in this text, it is nonetheless impressive that Zechariah places Messiah's coming within this general time frame. The New Testament specifically identifies the fulfillment of Zechariah 9:9 as the triumphal entry of Christ into Jerusalem at the beginning of what became the week of His passion (Matt. 21:5; John 12:15).

In this well-known text Zechariah makes four key statements about the coming King. Unfortunately, the implications of these statements are frequently overlooked because of the remarkable precision of the New Testament's application of the verse to Christ's riding a borrowed donkey into Jerusalem. We certainly do not want to ignore the obvious, specific fulfillment, but neither do we want to ignore the whole message, all of which applies to Christ.

First, *He is the promised King.* Zechariah's announcement, "Behold, thy King cometh unto thee," went to the heart of the Davidic covenant promise. Remember that

when Zechariah preached, David's throne was vacant. But
the prophet aimed the eye of faith beyond the empty throne
to the sure promise. That the prophet referred to "*thy*
King," using the second person singular pronoun, individ-
ualized the promise. The pronoun used in the King James
Version may be antiquated and foreign to modern usage,
but it enables the English reader to see what the Hebrew
reader saw. Christ's coming would indeed have national
and even worldwide relevance, but it had personal application to each believer. This was the long-awaited King
of promise. The prospect of seeing that King warranted
the admonition to rejoice: "Rejoice greatly, O daughter of
Zion; shout, O daughter of Jerusalem." Although both of
the imperatives carry the idea of shrieking loudly, one with
joy and the other with triumph, they express the inner celebration as well as any outward evidence of it. Nothing can
bring greater joy to a saint's heart than the personal Christ.
Whether then or now, it is a believing sight of Christ that
satisfies the heart.

Second, *He is the righteous King.* Zechariah marked as
one of the perfections of the promised king that "he is just."
Not only is Christ eternally and perfectly righteous by virtue of His deity, but He was animated with righteousness
throughout His earthly mission, and He will forever execute
righteousness in His royal authority. It was part of the messianic ideal that the Davidic king would judge His people
with righteousness and that righteousness would flourish
in His days (see especially 2 Sam. 23:3; Ps. 72:2, 7). Righteousness will burgeon during the kingdom reign of Christ;
however, since this verse refers specifically to Christ's first

advent, this righteousness most likely designates the positive and active obedience that the Lord performed during His earthly life. In every way the Lord Jesus satisfied the expectations and demands of the ideal King.

Third, *He is the victorious King*. This coming King is "having salvation." The meaning of this statement is disputed. The Hebrew text has a form of the verb "to save," which can convey either a passive sense of "being saved or delivered" or a stative sense of "being victorious." The Septuagint, the Greek translation of the Old Testament, and other ancient versions suggest the active sense of "one who saves," a Savior. Although either the active or the passive sense would accurately apply to the Messiah, the Hebrew text is preferable. That God's Messiah King is the object of divine help and deliverance is a recurring theme both in messianic prophecy (see Pss. 18:50; 20:6; 21:1, 4–5; 22:8) and in the earthly experience of Jesus recorded in the Gospels. From His deliverance as an infant from the plot of Herod, to His preservation in Gethsemane from Satan's last attempt to prevent the crucifixion, God saved the King from premature death. The greatest deliverance of all was His deliverance from the grave by the power of God in approval and vindication of His perfect life and atoning death. His deliverance marked His victory over every enemy and His ability and right to subdue every foe. His deliverance guarantees the salvation of all His people. Because He has been delivered, He is victorious, and He delivers and saves His people.

Fourth, *He is the humble King*. Finally, Zechariah describes the coming King as being "lowly." This word refers to more than the Messiah's poverty and meekness of spirit; it has the idea of being afflicted or oppressed and encompasses the whole suffering life of Christ. Zechariah's use of this word for the King closely parallels Isaiah's earlier description of the servant as being void of majesty, despised, and rejected (Isa. 53:2–5). Although Jesus was King, in His first incarnate appearance only the eye of faith could discern His royalty. That unbelief failed to see His kingship condemns the blindness of the heart; it does not alter the truth that Christ came as the King of kings. Messiah's riding "upon an ass, *even* upon the colt the foal of an ass," further defines His humble obedience (Zech. 9:9). Note, by the way, my translation of "even" rather than "and." This explicative or explanatory use of the conjunction is common and here is necessary to avoid the notion that Christ was riding two animals. The specific idea is that He was riding a young donkey, and this is the specific element of the prophecy that was fulfilled at the triumphal entry. The significance is not that the donkey was a lowly creature in contrast to the stately horse. Indeed, both the Old Testament and documents from the ancient Near East demonstrate that donkeys were often mounts for royalty and rulers (see Judg. 5:10; 10:4; 12:14; 2 Sam. 16:1–2). The people's response when they saw Christ riding into Jerusalem on the donkey was not surprise because a king was on a donkey. Rather, when they saw Him they immediately cried, "Blessed is the King of Israel that cometh in the name of the Lord" (John 12:13). For a king to ride a donkey was not contrary to expectation. The significance rests, rather, in that the Old Testament associated horses, war machines (see 9:10 where horses are associated with chariots and battle bows), with self-reliance and distrust of God (see Pss. 20:7; 33:16–17). If anything characterized Messiah's first coming, it was His faithful, unwavering dependence on God. Furthermore, God's initial instructions concerning kings prohibited their multiplying horses (Deut. 17:16). It would be aberrant for the ideal King, who was righteous in every other way, to associate Himself with that which marked kingly disobedience. Even in the detail of the donkey, Christ fulfilled all righteousness.

His Conquering

The coming King was the conquering King. The authority of any king or government is confined within its national borders. Those to whom Zechariah was ministering had recently been under the domination of the Babylonian Empire and were now subject to Persia. As powerful and authoritarian as those two kingdoms were, there were lines that marked the boundaries of domains. Amazingly, Zechariah said of the coming King, "He shall speak peace unto the heathen [nations]: and his dominion shall be from sea even to sea, and from the river even to the ends of the earth" (9:10). Later, he forthrightly declared, "And the LORD shall be king over all the earth" (14:9). That Christ's kingdom is without borders (9:10) is a source of great confidence. A king's authority is always limited by the borders of His kingdom, so a borderless kingdom speaks of unlimited authority. Kingdoms come and go because kings cannot hold on to what little they govern, but Christ's kingdom is without threat, for every human government exists with the borders of His. He rules all for His own glory and the good of His people. To be a citizen of His kingdom is reason for joy (9:17).

Not only is it reason for joy; it is also cause for hope. Significantly, it is in this context of the coming King whose rule is universal that Zechariah implores the "prisoners of hope" (9:12; i.e., the prisoners who have hope) to take their refuge in the stronghold (the King Himself). Greece was coming and Rome after them, but the King was coming irresistibly, "conquering, and to conquer" (Rev. 6:2). He conquers either by grace or with the rod of iron, but conquer He does.

This two-edged sword of grace and iron is evident in how the Lord accomplishes deliverance for His people. Consider this from Zechariah 12:8–10:

> In that day shall the LORD defend the inhabitants of Jerusalem…and the house of David shall be as God, as the angel of the LORD before them. And it shall come to pass in that day, that I will seek to destroy all the nations that come against Jerusalem. And I will pour upon the house of David, and upon the inhabitants of Jerusalem, the spirit of grace and of supplications.

On the one hand, destruction comes on the enemy—that is the rod of iron. On the other hand, a spiritual awakening comes on the covenant people—that is grace. Significantly, the execution of this iron-and-grace work is in connection with "the house of David," which would be as God and the Angel of the Lord. Since the next ruler from David's house would be Messiah Himself, this is unmistakably detailing the conquest of the coming King.

In this passage and often in the final section of Zechariah's prophecy (chapters 9–14), the prophet puts this unfailing conquest in the context of "that day," an abbreviation of the fuller expression the "Day of the Lord" (2:11; 3:10; 9:16; 12:3, 4, 6, 8, 9, 11; 13:1, 2, 4; 14:4, 6, 8, 9, 13, 20, 21; the full expression in 14:1, 7). The Day of the Lord is a common prophetic theme, perhaps originating with Obadiah, the earliest of the writing prophets (mid-ninth century BC). The word "day" does not refer to a twenty-four-hour period; it is a temporal word to designate those epoch interventions of God into the affairs of time and circumstance. In contrast to providence, which is the ordinary work of God by which He governs and preserves all His creation, the Day of the Lord is an extraordinary act of God when He breaks into time in spectacular fashion either to judge the wicked or to deliver the righteous. I often define the Day of the Lord in terms of eternity breaking into time.[3]

The conquering of the King reaches its climax in Zechariah 14. At the moment when everything seems to be hopeless, with every hostile force of the world gathered against God's people (14:2), the King appears, taking His stand on the Mount of Olives (14:4). He comes at the place He is needed most, and when He comes, nothing remains the same. He defeats every enemy (14:3), either with the plague (14:12) or with grace turning the Gentile survivors into worshipers of the King, the LORD of Hosts (14:16). Sin is subdued; the curse is reversed with the distinction between the sacred and secular disappearing (14:20–21). The King will make everything better than ever imagined.

Granted, the scene described is subject to various views of the end times. Confessedly, the details and the timing can be confusing. Nonetheless, the overriding and inescapable message is that there is a happy hope for all believers that God and Christ will triumph. The day is coming when every vestige of sin will be gone and the unrelenting power of the gospel to reverse the effects of the curse will be manifest. For Zechariah to end his prophecy this way justifies his reputation as being the prophet of hope—a hope that he squarely focuses on Christ, the ideal Prophet, Priest, and King.

QUESTIONS

1. How does messianic kingship/sovereignty differ from divine kingship/sovereignty?

2. Summarize the meaning of the four titles of Christ in 10:4 and think about how each applies specifically to you.

3. Note the significance of the reference to "thy King" in 9:9 and reflect on the implications of that to you.

4. What does the Hebrew verb translated "having salvation" in 9:9 teach about Christ?

5. What does Christ's being called "lowly" in 9:9 teach about Him?

6. What is the significance of Christ's riding on the donkey?

7. Why is the word "day" used in the expression "Day of the Lord" if it doesn't refer to a twenty-four-hour period?

13

The Fulfillment of Hope: Generally Speaking

Some of what Zechariah prophesied has been fulfilled in time; some remains to be fulfilled in the end of time. Yet-to-be fulfilled prophecy is just as certain as already fulfilled prophecy; the only difference is the point on the time line of God's eternal and unstoppable plan. It is as certain before its realization as it is after it. The details of realized prophecy may be more in focus, but not the essential substance. What has been fulfilled only fuels faith in God's fidelity and His ability to do whatever He says He is going to do. Although there is no doubt regarding the certainty of God's word, there should be an intensifying desire for its materialization, an eager expectancy for its actual, in-time fulfillment. That is what hope is all about, and it is only natural that postponed or delayed expectancy should cause a yearning that can ultimately be satisfied only when the future becomes the now (see Prov. 13:12). The sad fact of the matter is that so many Christians can read about the future God has purposed for His glory and His people's good with a cold complacency rather than with a burning yearning to experience its reality. John exemplifies the pattern we all should follow. In response to Christ's certain affirmation, "Surely I come quickly. Amen," John expressed his yearning, "Even so, come, Lord Jesus" (Rev. 22:20).

So even though not every point of Zechariah's hopeful message has transitioned into time, it is just a matter of time before it does. Consequently, I've titled this chapter that will summarize some of Zechariah's chief prophecies "The Fulfillment of Hope." Reflecting on what God's certain "then" will look like when fulfilled is a principal means of keeping hope alive. The certain fulfillment of prophecy should never breed passivity or fatalistic resignation to "whatever will be, will be." On the contrary, it should encourage believers to confident engagement in kingdom service and move both saints and sinners to repentance and purity. Zechariah projected hope as a means of progressing the work of the kingdom. Zechariah 8:9 expresses that objective well: "Let your hands be strong, ye that hear in these days these words by the mouth of the prophets." The people in those days who heard did not actually see or experience the realization of some of what they heard, but not seeing the fulfillment did not diminish the hope of its certain fulfillment. What the fulfillment would look like was incentive enough to live in its reality. That application remains for all who read his prophecy.

Rather than isolating and exegeting specific texts throughout the book, I want to make my point by highlighting the content and symbolic significance of Zechariah's opening visions. These visions in many ways provide a panoramic overview of God's overarching purpose and plan that the prophet then delineates with specifics, particularly in the final section of the book (chapters 9–14).

My concern is to demonstrate in broad terms how Zechariah develops his theology of hope. But I can't resist at least highlighting the salient features of this final section, some of which we already considered in the discussions of Christ, the focus of hope.

The final section of Zechariah's prophecy (chapters 9–14), dating about thirty-five years after the completion of the temple, which was the prophet's initial concern, delineates in sometimes apocalyptic tones what the Lord was going to do to reverse the fortunes of His people who remained subject to Persian rule. This final section consists of two prophetic oracles of blessing. The first oracle (chapters 9–11) predicts judgment on enemies, the coming messianic King, and the rejected shepherd. The second (chapters 12–14) points to a national and spiritual deliverance in connection with the coming Messiah. Significantly, Zechariah's before-the-fact description of the anticipated fulfillment of God's purpose included both physical and spiritual deliverances.

Often in terms of the Day of the Lord, those epoch interventions of God into time and circumstance, the prophet predicts the defeat of every enemy. Having gathered all the nations together for battle, the Lord shall "go forth, and fight against those nations, as when he fought in the day of battle" (14:2–3). The final display of those divine victories is summed up in terms of the universal recognition of divine authority and reputation: "And the LORD shall be king over all the earth: in that day shall there be one LORD, and his name one" (14:9). Zechariah proffers the hope that traditional enemies, such as Syria and Philistia

(9:1–6), and yet to be enemies, such as Greece (9:13), would suffer defeat by divine intervention. In a remarkable turn of providence, the nation that for centuries already had paid and for centuries to come would pay tribute to foreign governments would be the repository of the world's wealth: "The wealth of all the heathen round about shall be gathered together, gold, and silver, and apparel, in great abundance" (14:14). Things were going to get a lot better than they had ever experienced. Keeping the end in sight was key to living the daily way by faith. They knew what was going to happen; they just did not know when. It is the certainty of fulfillment that keeps hope active.

Even more significant than the deliverances from physical bondage would be the effecting of spiritual transformations, all of which would be consequent to the Messiah's coming and work—the focus of hope. The regenerating work of the Holy Spirit would open blinded eyes to the reality of the Messiah's atoning work, producing a godly sorrow: "And I will pour upon the house of David, and upon the inhabitants of Jerusalem, the spirit of grace and of supplications: and they shall look upon me whom they have pierced, and they shall mourn for him" (12:10). When God pours out His Spirit, dispensing grace and generating prayer, He shows the power and consequence of regeneration. The Spirit awakens the sinner to look with understanding on Christ (the One who was pierced) and then to seek favor from God. On the basis of Messiah's work, the Lord graciously would open a fountain "for sin and for uncleanness" (13:1). Pointedly, this reference to the cleansing fountain comes between the reference to

Messiah's being pierced by men (12:10) and His being the
target of God's sword (13:7). It is as though Zechariah here
is the voice anticipating Peter's Pentecostal sermon speaking of Christ: "Him, being delivered by the determinate
counsel and foreknowledge of God, ye have taken, and by
wicked hands have crucified and slain" (Acts 2:23).

Indications are that this spiritual awakening is not limited to Israel. But this should not be surprising because
the promise of Messiah in the Old Testament was never a
uniquely Jewish promise. Although the human lineage of
Christ would come through Israel, the significance of His
work was worldwide, for it was in Abraham's Seed that all
the families of the earth were going to be blessed (Gen.
12:3). That Gentiles are included in the spiritual awakening is suggested by the survivors of the nations (those not
conquered by the divine sword but rather conquered by
grace) participating in the worship of the King, the Lord
of Hosts, including the celebration of the Feast of Tabernacles (14:16). This feast commemorates God's presence and
providential protection of His people. Here it represents
the whole of divinely prescribed and acceptable worship by
both Jew and Gentile. The Feast of Tabernacles, memorial-
izing the wilderness experience, symbolized what it meant
to depend wholly on the Lord. Depending on God for all
the necessities of physical life (food and water) pictures the
far more important issue of depending on God for all that
is necessary for spiritual life, Christ who is both the living
bread and water for His people.

The bottom line is that Zechariah's prospect for the
future seemed in so many ways to be too good to be true.

Things were going to be so different from what the people were currently experiencing. Zechariah 8 paints a scene of blessing that illustrates the point. This is part of the prophet's answer to a question whether fasting to commemorate Jerusalem's fall to the Babylonians was still in order, given that the exile was now over (7:1–3). The prophet first answers the question by assessing the fasts as hypocritical (7:4–7) and then arguing that obedience is far better than any heartless rituals (7:8–14). He next turns their attention away from the fast-causing circumstances to a time when devastation would give way to restoration (8:1–17) and mourning would be replaced with joy (8:18–23). The fulfillment of the blessing would include the Lord's presence (8:3), peace (8:3–5), prosperity (8:11–12), and piety (8:3). So dramatic the reversal will be that the sad fast will give way to a cheerful feast filled with joy and gladness (8:19). So attractive will the blessing be that Gentiles will seek the Lord and join in true worship (8:22–23) in a worldwide revival of true religion. All these blessings heaped on one another defy comprehension. But the incomprehensible should not foster doubt but rather a confident hope in the Lord and His infinite ability. The Lord graciously gave the assurance that the magnitude of the blessing should not be a hindrance to belief: "Thus saith the LORD of hosts; If it be marvellous in the eyes of the remnant of this people in these days, should it also be marvellous in mine eyes? saith the LORD of hosts" (8:6). That the question is framed by the Lord of Hosts, Zechariah's most common designation for the Lord, adds to the certainty of the implied answer. Making the promises was the Commander in Chief who had all creation at His disposal to order and accomplish His will; nothing or no one could frustrate His eternal purpose. The word translated "marvellous" means difficult, or beyond one's power; it often refers to God's extraordinary and miraculous acts. What was incomprehensible and humanly impossible to accomplish was not in any way beyond God's will to purpose or His ability to perform. Nothing is too hard for the Lord; indeed, nothing is hard for Him at all. Because God made the promises, the fulfillment was certain. The timing is as much a part of His plan as the circumstances. So even though aspects of fulfillment are not yet, the remnant then and the church now must labor for the kingdom with diligence (8:9) and live with the certain hope that all will be as God has planned.

Although the scene described in Zechariah 14 is subject to various views of the end times, it does generate the happy hope for all believers that God, Christ, and truth will triumph. A new heaven and new earth are coming that will be free from every vestige of sin and will manifest the power of the gospel in reversing the curse. The desire of every believer should be "Even so, come, Lord Jesus" (Rev. 22:20). The way Zechariah closes his prophecy justifies his reputation as the prophet of hope.

And yet I cannot leave these general remarks without a word of exhortation. God's plan and purpose are certain and cannot be frustrated; consequently, there is hope for all believers. That is the point. Personal enjoyment and experience of God's redemptive purpose require individual faith and repentance. Zechariah makes it clear from the beginning of his prophecy that the realization of hope is conditioned by repentance: "Therefore say thou unto them,

Thus saith the LORD of hosts; Turn ye unto me, saith the LORD of hosts, and I will turn unto you, saith the LORD of hosts" (1:3). The verb meaning "to turn" is the principal word used in the Old Testament for evangelical repentance. It means to reverse directions. When sinners turn away from their sins and turn toward the Lord, the Lord will graciously receive them with mercy. God, in Christ, has made the way to reverse the curse for all who come to Him (John 6:37). So as we reflect on the grand things God has in store for His people, let us make sure that we are among His people. "Turn ye to me, saith the Lord of hosts." That is the hope that is the anchor of the soul (Heb. 6:19).

QUESTIONS

1. What should be the proper and primary application of yet-to-be fulfilled prophecy? How does the promise of Christ's return affect you?

2. Explain how Zechariah illustrates the truth of Acts 2:23.

3. Why is the Feast of Tabernacles a fitting symbol of the future universal worship of the true God?

4. Although God's redemptive purpose is certain, what is the condition for personal enjoyment and experience of it?

5. What image is suggested by the Hebrew word for repentance? How has your life mirrored that image?

14

The Fulfillment of Hope:
Figuratively Speaking

One of the ways God revealed Himself and His word before the completion of the inspired canon was through visions. It was common among the prophets and most certainly was a key means by which God revealed the message of hope to Zechariah. Although visions were something prophets saw internally and individually, they nonetheless constituted and came with the authority of the word of the Lord. Zechariah makes that link clearly: "In the second year of Darius, came the word of the LORD unto Zechariah…the prophet, saying" (1:7), and then Zechariah immediately says, "I saw by night" (1:8). In a series of eight visions that seemed to occur in uninterrupted procession in that single night, God overviewed His redemptive plan and purpose from the immediate temporal context to the distant future. By inspiration Zechariah's personal visions have transitioned to the written Word.

As we read what Zechariah saw, we will be confronted with some of the same issues that he confronted. Visions employ figurative language and are highly symbolic. There were times when Zechariah had to confess to the interpreting angel present to guide him through the visions that he did not quite understand the significance of what he was seeing (4:4–5). But the divinely given interpreter kept him focused on the salient points, as in Zechariah 1:9, where the angel says, "I will show thee what these be." That's what I want to do as well. Admittedly, figurative and symbolic language involves some degree of subjectivity in the interpretative process and requires using the imagination to identify the principal point. But engaging the imagination does not equate to unrestrained or borderless speculation. The context frames thought. In deciphering the symbols, it is important to discern what is incidental and what is integral to the message. So without commenting on every detail, I want to identify the key thoughts in Zechariah's visions. Simply said, I want us to see the picture and get the point. Some will require a more detailed synopsis than others, but together they will provide a panoramic view, the big picture, of what the realization or fulfillment of hope is going to look like. Even without the details of how things will happen, it is unmistakably clear and certain that all will transpire to God's glory and the good of His people. God removes every obstacle standing in the way of His purpose—whether inward or external, whether spiritual or physical. The certain fulfillment generates hope, and that is good: "It is good that a man should both hope and quietly wait for the salvation of the LORD" (Lam. 3:26).

Vision 1: The Reversal of Fortunes

The principal parts of the first vision (1:7–17) are a man on a red horse stationed among some myrtle trees located in a ravine or hollow and surrounded by multicolored horses. The immediate questions concern the identity of the man, his location among the myrtles, the significance of the horses, and what the man is doing. Ultimately, what the man is doing is the main point of the picture that creates the foundation for the hope that there was going be a reversal of fortunes. Things are going to get better for God's people and worse for their oppressors.

Verse 11 explicitly identifies the man standing among the myrtles as the Angel of the Lord. By Zechariah's time there had been multiple appearances of the Angel, and those antecedent appearances inform both Zechariah's and our understanding of who He is. The fact that I'm using a capital letter is a hint as to His identity. The expression could be translated "the Messenger who is Jehovah" and is a common title in the Old Testament to refer to a christophany. A christophany is a preincarnate appearance of the Son of God. *Preincarnate* designates the time before the eternal Son took to Himself human flesh. Christophanies were occasions when the Second Person of the Holy Trinity appeared as a man, but was not a man. He took the form of man (outward appearance), but not the nature of man (the essence of being). He appeared with a message—hence, the title "angel," which literally has the idea of messenger. I am also suggesting that the reference "of Jehovah" should be understood as an appositional statement. Apposition is when a second noun renames the first, usually in more specific terms. So the Messenger (the general name) is Jehovah (the specific name). There are times when the Messenger is definitely identified as God, possessing divine perfections or performing divine works. Yet there are times when the

Messenger is distinct from God. The principal evidence for this is that the Angel, who often speaks as Jehovah in the first person, also speaks of Jehovah in the third person. The Old Testament references to the Angel are as complex as the Trinity itself, and that is the point. This christophany was an effective, unmistakable means of revelation whereby God not only made Himself known but also introduced the unique person who would be the only One in whom the invisible God would be visible.[4]

Although Zechariah saw the same angel that appeared externally to Hagar, Abraham, Moses, and all the rest before him, what he saw does not technically constitute a christophany. That is, it was not an actual appearance of the preincarnate Christ on the earth. It was a real manifestation of the same angel, but it was revealed to the inner consciousness of the prophet. What Zechariah saw was real, but he saw it in himself and not in front of him; the vision was internal, not external. As far as he was concerned, it was a christophany indeed, and the implications of that are integral to the message. Zechariah's vision of the Angel of the Lord provides a foretaste of Messiah's priestly function.

Before I explain that statement, I need to comment briefly on the other principal parts of the vision. Admittedly, interpreting the other components is more subjective since the text does not identify them as it does the man among the myrtles. But keeping within the contextual boundaries, here is what I would suggest. The myrtle trees in the bottom or hollow represent the nation of Israel, fragrant but lowly. This would be a fitting picture of the nation, representing their low estate and unfortunate condition as they had returned from the captivity to a city still bearing the marks of its devastating ruins. The multicolored horses represent a host of angels, those ministering spirits that are the agents of divine providence. Here, they were on a reconnaissance mission to discover the status of the nations, particularly those that afflicted Israel. Their report was that those nations were still and at rest (1:11); they were at peace and secure. In this context, it seems that the color of the horses is incidental since all are on the same mission and all give a unified report. Nonetheless, red may symbolize judgment, white victory, and speckled (sorrel or pale red, not spotted) a mixture of judgment and mercy. But the bottom line is that the text does not link any distinctive action to any particular color. It is probably best not to force the color issue.

It is what the Angel does with the horse report that points to His priestly function. His standing among the myrtle trees most likely represents His presence among the people: He identifies Himself with His people. That's one thing priests do. It parallels closely Isaiah's statement regarding the Angel during Israel's wilderness experience: "In all their affliction he was afflicted" (Isa. 63:9). But most significant is the Angel's interceding for this people. In verse 12, the Angel pleads with the Lord to show mercy on the nation by fully ending the seventy-year demonstration of divine indignation. Significantly, He intercedes on the basis of what the Lord had promised (see Jer. 25:12). Intercession is priestly work.

It is how the Lord answers the intercession that sets the course for hope. Whether intercession from the preincarnate Christ or the incarnate Christ, the prayers of Christ are always answered. That is the believer's solid hope; He ever lives to make intercession (Heb. 7:25). The application of that is far-reaching, but in this vision it involves the reversing of fortunes for God's people. The Lord declares His jealousy or fervent zeal for His people (1:14) and that the nations currently enjoying peace are the objects of His displeasure for overstepping the bounds of their commission as the agents of God's chastisement (1:15). God announced His return to Jerusalem with mercies (displays of compassion designed to alleviate a pitiable circumstance). Consequently, the nation, now in the valley, would prosper, and the nation once scattered in exile would expand their borders in peace (1:16–17).

The first vision does not detail how this reversal of fortune will occur, but the fact of restoration is divinely certain. The temple will be rebuilt, and the city will be restored (1:16). What will be is reason for hope.

Vision 2: Power Enough

The principal parts of the second vision (1:18–21, which is 2:1–4 in the Hebrew Bible) are the four horns and four carpenters. The picture is simple, and the point is explicitly explained. The point is that God has enough power to dispose of every force hostile to His purpose and His people. Horns (bull horns, not musical instruments) are commonly used in the Old Testament to designate strength or power. Here the horns refer specifically to the world powers or nations that are hostile to God's people. Rather than speculating as to the identity of four particular nations, it is best to recognize the symbolic significance of the number four as referring to the four corners of the world. Thus the four horns represent the enemies of God's people across the world.

The four carpenters or craftsmen are those that will rout the horns, driving them in terror and casting them down. Regardless of how powerful the horn may be, there is a craftsman to smash it. God has power enough to curb the advance of every enemy. He has infinite resources for the protection of His people. The purpose of this short vision is to elaborate on God's displeasure with the nations (1:15). It would appear that the hostile forces of this world are far superior and can so easily have their way against God's people. But the bottom line is that God's power is infinitely great, and no enemy is able to stand against it. Hope fulfilled means that every enemy of God and His kingdom will be defeated.

Vision 3: Blessing beyond Expectation

The principal scene of the third vision (2:1–13, which is 2:5–17 in the Hebrew Bible) is the man with a measuring line who attempts to measure the city limits of Jerusalem. The brevity and simplicity of the vision are countered with a detailed explanation and exhortation. What Zechariah sees in a vision is what Paul declared in doxology: "Now unto him that is able to do exceeding abundantly above all that we ask or think" (Eph. 3:20). God's blessing is beyond expectation. This is one of my favorite passages in Zechariah, and it can be summed up under three heads.

First, *God's purpose for His people is greater than expectations* (2:1–5). This statement is magnified in the light of faith's great expectations. The mission of the man with the measuring line was to mark the borders of Jerusalem. Most likely, this man represents the "everyman" who was expressing the common notions of the day, at least the notions of those who believed the prophetic word that Jerusalem was going to be restored (1:16–17; Jer. 29:10–14). To set out to measure the city limits at this time was no small demonstration of faith. The city was in ruins, and the temple was in shambles; the rubble of destruction cluttered the streets. Sight saw devastation; faith perceived restoration. Measuring the city was testimony to faith that God indeed would return in His jealousy and mercy to restore the city (1:14–17). But yet, to measure is to mark borders and to set limits. Here is the weakness of faith even in its exercise. Sometimes God's people are afraid to believe too much lest they become disappointed if He does not work according to their notions. Sadly, this is how so many of God's people seem to live. We know what God has said, and we believe it. Yet reason is often hindered by perception and experience, preventing us from appropriating the fullness of God's word and promise. No matter how much we believe, what we see has the power to rein in hope.

The next scene in the vision addresses that limitation by directing attention to God's greater purpose. The man with the measuring line is instructed to put up the ruler and not to bother measuring the city limits. Measuring the city at this juncture was premature because measuring the fullness of God's blessing is impossible. God's purpose transcends our limitations to fathom what He has in store for His people. City walls marked borders and constituted the chief defensive barrier against enemy attack. The fulfillment of God's purpose would mean that there would be no walls to measure because the population was going to be so immense that walls could not contain it; there would be no city limits (2:4). As well, no walls would be necessary for defensive purposes because God's presence would provide inviolable security: "For I, saith the LORD, will be unto her a wall of fire round about, and will be the glory in the midst of her" (2:5).

This is a vision of the success of grace. The implications of this kingdom expansion are remarkably wonderful and point to the climactic fulfillment of God's covenant promises. Here is the manifestation of the covenant promise to Abraham that he would be the father of a multitude (Gen. 12:2–3; 17:4) and a foretaste of heaven's population consisting of those from every people and language group on the face of the earth (Rev. 7:9). God's purpose was for a new and ideal Israel consisting of a citizenship from every ethnic group on the planet. God's people in every age are part of that plan of irresistible grace. Confessedly, I don't know how or when the climax of this fulfillment will be realized when we can see what we believe. But knowing that this is God's great plan and purpose should move us today, just as Zechariah wanted to move his generation, to active and bold confidence to walk by faith in the point on the time line that God has placed us. It should be our confession that we believe; it should be our prayer that God would help our unbelief (Mark 9:24).

Second, *God's protection of His people inspires confidence for duty* (2:6–9). The rest of the chapter delineates the corollary applications of the vision itself, particularly with its focus on God's presence with and protection of His people. With logic anticipating Paul's, Zechariah demands that duty must flow from truth. This section addresses specifically the theme of divine protection.

The imagery of verse 8 clearly states the fact of God's protection: "He that toucheth you toucheth the apple of his eye." The apple of the eye is the gate or opening of the eye, referring to the pupil. The eye is sensitive to touch and consequently is the object of special care. The point is that God's people are special to Him, and He is sensitive to what threatens them. Very graphically in anthropomorphic terms, to touch God's people in hostility is tantamount to poking God in the eye. It is an amazing truth that believers are so special to the Lord.

The particular agent of this protection is Christ Himself. Comparing verses 8 and 9, notwithstanding some surface confusion, reveals some profound theology. Here is the surface confusion: in verse 8 the Lord of Hosts speaks, saying, "After the glory hath he sent me unto the nations which spoiled you." He continues with the assurance that He will turn the spoilers into spoil so that "ye shall know that the LORD of hosts hath sent me" (2:9). On the one hand, the Lord of Hosts is the one being sent, and on the other hand, the Lord of Hosts does the sending. Admittedly, this is confusing and seemingly contradictory, but theologically it profoundly points to the trinitarian mystery; the title

Lord of Hosts (Commander in Chief) designates both the Father and the Son.

Remember that as Messiah, the divinely appointed and anointed Mediator, Christ functions as prophet, priest, and king. His special commission in this text highlights His kingly work as He conquers all of His and His people's enemies. As the Commander in Chief (Lord of Hosts) he reveals His mission: "After the glory hath he sent me unto the nations which spoiled you" (2:8). The statement is a bit cryptic, but the sense is clear enough. In pursuit of glory, to reveal or accomplish glory, He will turn the tables. The spoilers will become the spoiled by His shaking His hand, an image for the effective brandishing and wielding the sword (2:9). The glory being pursued is undoubtedly God's glory that will be manifest in the midst of His people (2:5). This is in keeping with Messiah's mission as the Lord Jesus confessed to His Father when His earthly mission was drawing to a close: "I have glorified thee on the earth: I have finished the work which thou gavest me to do" (John 17:4). The key thought for the encouragement of God's people then and for God's people now is that Christ is active in their behalf. That was true before and after the incarnation. It remains true that the incarnate Christ, although not physically present on earth, is ruling His kingdom absolutely, to the end that all the earth will be filled with both the knowledge and glory of God just as the waters fill the sea (Hab. 2:14). What rebels and enemies there may be are doomed and destined to destruction.

That is not only cause for hope for the future but reason for living well in Christ's kingdom now. The proper response to the Lord's certain protection is to separate from the world that is sentenced to judgment. Since God's people are the part of the world destined for glory, they should not grow comfortable in the world destined to pass away. Using verbal exclamation marks ("Ho, ho") to get their attention, Zechariah punctuates the divine impera- tive to "flee from the land of the north" (2:6). He then explicitly says, "Deliver thyself, O Zion, that dwellest with the daughter of Babylon" (2:7). Since most invasions into Israel came from the north, that compass point designated the enemy regardless of the geographical location of the kingdom itself. So even though Babylon was east of Jeru- salem, at that time it was the "north" land because it was the enemy that had destroyed Jerusalem and had taken so many captive. It is true that Jeremiah had instructed those taken into captivity to carry on with their lives by build- ing houses, planting gardens, raising families, and living peaceably (Jer. 29:4–7). But he had also made it clear that at the end of seventy years, Babylon was going to suffer perpetual desolation because of its iniquity (Jer. 25:12). Zechariah is preaching after those seventy years. Some of the exiles had returned home, but some remained in Babylon. They had become comfortable as captives, having apparently followed Jeremiah's survival formula but failing to heed his warning. Zechariah directs his exhortation to those still living in Babylon to leave because God's purpose to bless His people was so magnificently great and they needed to identify themselves with those God intended to bless, not with those He intended to curse. God's purpose was to spread them abroad as the four winds (2:6). This is not a dispersing in judgment like the exile. Rather, the image is the spreading of a garment to claim possession of whatever it covers. It is foolish for God's people to side with the world that is passing away when they should be living in the reality of God's blessing and taking possession of the inheritance that is purposed for them.

We can easily put Zechariah's exhortation to separate from the world in New Testament terms. John admonishes believers to "love not the world, neither the things that are in the world" since "the world passeth away" (1 John 2:15, 17). Similarly, Paul commands in the light of God's dwelling with believers to "come out from among them, and be ye separate, saith the Lord, and touch not the unclean thing" (2 Cor. 6:16–17). After all, "what fellowship hath righteousness with unrighteousness?" (2 Cor. 6:14).

Third, *God's presence with His people is reason for joy* (2:10–13). This final section expands on the promise of the divine presence: "For, lo, I come, and I will dwell in the midst of thee, saith the LORD" (2:10, 11). The word "dwell" is the verb root that is the basis for the references to God's *shekinah* glory. Although the word *shekinah* does not actually occur in the Old Testament, the concept of God's abiding presence is a frequent theme. It refers here to God's taking up His residence with His covenant people and the consequent enjoyment of fellowship and communion. God has manifested His presence in various ways, including the incarnation, and certainly we experience it now specifically in terms of the unceasing, abiding presence of the Holy Spirit in the hearts and lives of every believer. But as the New Testament explains for us, as good as this presence is, it is only the down payment of that which is inconceivably better—the fullness of blessing in heavenly places (Eph. 1:14, 3, respectively). Significantly, Zechariah points to a time when Christ's mediatorial kingdom extends to the Gentiles, who will become the Lord's people and will experience God's abiding covenantal presence (2:11). But the inclusion of the Gentiles does not exclude the Jews (2:12). All this is what the apostle Paul so wonderfully explained in Ephesians 2:12–21. Gentiles, who were strangers to the covenant and without hope, have been reconciled and made one with the covenant people, the middle wall of partition having been abolished in Christ, who made all His people one. Every conversion is evidence of God's great purpose being on track to its ultimate fulfillment.

There is little wonder, then, why Zechariah says, "Sing and rejoice, O daughter of Zion" (2:10). Singing has the idea of lifting the voice with a shout; the heart expression is more important than the tune. *Rejoicing* is a word of jubilation, referring to the praise and worship directed to the Lord. Joy to the world indeed—because the Lord has come and will come again in the fullness of glory.

The concluding admonition of this vision is fitting: "Be silent, O all flesh, before the LORD: for he is raised up out of his holy habitation" (2:13). "Be silent" is actually an interjection meaning "hush," or as we might indicate by putting our finger over our lips and breathing "sh." Calm down with thoughts about the Lord's purpose, protection, and presence. Regardless of what we may see in the world, the Lord is about to be stirred to set all in motion. He will get all glory; every enemy will be spoiled; and every believer will own His Lord and share in covenant promise and blessing. The prospects are good.

Vision 4: Salvation from Sin

The first three visions have set before the people the hope of national deliverance and prosperity, a hope that was certain and authenticated by the word of the Lord. Yet the spiritually minded, particularly, would have been conscious that their personal holiness did not merit such grandiose promises. And they would have been correct. The basis of favor was not in their merits; the basis was God's grace. So this fourth vision narrows from national to individual focus and addresses the very personal issue of salvation from sin.

The principal scene of this fourth vision centers on Joshua the high priest. Since the high priest was the paramount representative of the people of God, we must see him here not only in terms of his own person but also in terms of his office. What is true of Joshua is true for every justified sinner. That is the ultimate point of the vision as it symbolically pictures the gospel truth of free and gracious justification. As we meditate on this vision, keep in mind the classic Reformed and biblically precise definition of justification in the Westminster Shorter Catechism: "Justification is an act of God's free grace, wherein he pardoneth all our sins, and accepteth us as righteous in his sight, only for the righteousness of Christ imputed to us, and received by faith alone" (Q. 33). This vision is instructive to teach sinners what must be done if they are to be plucked from the burning (3:2); it is instructive to saints to remind them that none can lay anything to the charge of God's elect because it is God who justifies (Rom. 8:33). Four essential components of justification are pictured in the vision. They say that a picture is worth a thousand words. That may or may not be true, but here is a picture that is worth a soul.

First, the need for justification is great. The passage begins with a judicial scene in which Joshua, the accused, is standing before the Angel of the Lord, the judge, and is being accused by Satan, the prosecutor. *Satan* literally means "the accuser" or "adversary" and is a noun form of the verb translated here "to resist." In other words, Satan was being Satan, or the accuser was accusing. He is the great adversary who accuses God to us (Gen. 3:1–5) and accuses us to God (see Job 1–2). The specific accusation against Joshua is not recorded, but can be inferred from how Joshua is dressed (3:3). It is an accurate picture of how every man on his own stands before God. He stands silently, dressed in detestably filthy garments, with no self-defense before the Judge. The language is graphic in describing the garments as heinously detestable and disgusting, fouled by excrement and vomit. The sight is not pretty, but it vividly pictures how man appears before God in all the filthy rags of his own righteousness; it is a true and accurate picture of the sinner's moral pollution. Because of unrighteousness, all men are guilty before the just God. That part of Satan's accusation was true because man has no inherent right to stand before God and to be accepted on his own merit. Joshua's vile condition cries for something to be done. It requires a free justification just as Paul argues: because all have sinned, God must justify freely or there could be no justification (see the logic of Rom. 3:23–24).

Second, the act of justification is gracious. Joshua was silent; he offered no self-defense; he was guilty as charged. But the vision highlights something of the beauty of the gospel in that God does for man what man cannot do for himself. Seemingly out of the blue, God rebukes Satan and rescues Joshua as a brand plucked from the burning. He was fit for destruction but delivered by grace. Joshua was accepted before the Lord and allowed to stand in His presence. The accuser was swept away; he had no power to condemn the one that God accepts (see Rom. 8:31–39). The text highlights two essential elements of that acceptance. First, the Lord graciously pardoned sin. This is pictured by the removal of the filthy garments and explained directly: "I have caused thine iniquity to pass from thee" (3:4). The guilt and, therefore, the liability for punishment and penalty were removed. But taking away the filthy garments alone would only result in nakedness before God and the susceptibility to fouling things up again. Something positive had to be done. Second, the Lord provided righteousness. Not only were the filthy garments removed, but they were replaced with costly and glorious clothes. The "fair mitre" refers to the headdress of the high priest engraved with "HOLINESS TO THE LORD" (Ex. 28:36). The filth was replaced by radiating holiness, without which no man can see God. This represents that "robe of righteousness," the "garments of salvation" (Isa. 61:10) that renders the wearer presentable before the Lord. In justification, God both pardons sin and imputes the righteousness of Christ.

Third, the ground of justification is solid. God's pardoning sinners is gracious, but it is not capricious. This brings us to the Branch (3:8). We've already considered the Branch as the focus of hope in chapter 11, so I'm not going to repeat that discussion. But we do need to put it in the context of this picture of justification. It is the Lord's sending the Branch that would be the meritorious grounds by which He justifies sinners. That the Branch is called the servant, charged with all Isaiah's servant theology, speaks of His humble obedience both in life and to death. I would suggest the reference to iniquity's being removed in one day (3:9) points to His cross, the only place where iniquity was effectively removed. Christ's perfect life (His active obedience) and His effectual death (His passive obedience) are the only meritorious ground for salvation.

Fourth, the demand of justification is logical. Zechariah makes it clear that a change in legal standing demands a change in moral behavior. A change in standing demands a change in walking. Justification always issues in sanctification; position always affects experience. Grace never leaves a man where it finds him. Those justified are to persevere in godliness by walking in God's ways (a manner of life conforming to God's law), keeping His charge (obedience and fidelity to God's ordinances), and maintaining justice (3:7). Those justified are to be like Christ; they are to imitate and represent Him. Zechariah described Joshua and his fellows as "men wondered at" (3:8). Literally, they were "men of a sign," men who were to be types of something else; they were to signify the Branch. So it is that every justified sinner is to be like Christ, to be conformed to His image. These implications of justification would make a pretty good sermon!

The vision begins with a picture of despair coming from a condemning heart that too often hears the accusations of the accuser. It ends with the assurance and hope that God will remove every obstacle to blessing for His people, even the sin that separates from Him (Isa. 59:2). The vision illustrates John's declaration that "if our heart condemn us, God is greater than our heart" (1 John 3:20). Rather than being abandoned to the fire (3:2), God's people are as a stone upon which are seven eyes (3:9). Opinions differ as to what this means, but I would suggest that the stone represents the Lord's people, His kingdom, upon or toward which He directs His seven eyes, a symbol of His omniscience and consequent protecting care. They will also enjoy, because of the work of the Branch, peace and prosperity. This is the point of the symbolism in verse 10 of calling every man neighbor (peace) and residing under the vine and fig tree (prosperity). God has the answers to all our concerns, both corporate and individual. What He has promised that seems to be too good to be true is not. His providing the means for salvation from sin by the Branch assures us that everything else He has promised is sure. Paul put it this way: "He that spared not his own Son, but delivered him up for us all, how shall he not with him also freely give us all things?"(Rom. 8:32).

Vision 5: Power for Service

Whereas the fourth vision focused on Joshua, the church leader, the fifth vision focuses on Zerubbabel, the civil leader. Whereas the fourth vision addressed the removal of the internal obstacle of sin by the work of the Branch

(Christ), the fifth vision addresses the removal of every external obstacle to the advance of the kingdom by the work of the Holy Spirit. There is salvation from sin, and there is power for service. Happily, the points of both visions are not limited to those two individuals.

The principal parts of this vision are the candlestick or lampstand that is situated between two olive trees with pipes or troughs funneling oil directly from the trees to the lampstand. Interpreting this picture requires factoring in some of the symbolism from the tabernacle and temple. There are some pictures within the picture. The picture, therefore, is a bit complex, but the point will be clear—thanks to Zechariah's interpreting angel.

Before addressing the unique features of Zechariah's lampstand that constitute the main point of the vision's message, I will consider the symbolism and typology of the lampstand. *Symbols* refer to object lessons designed to teach a spiritual truth to contemporaries. *Types* refer to the future realities that are being symbolized. Simply said, types are divinely given picture prophecies that will and must be fulfilled as certainly as any and every spoken or written prophecy.

The lampstand was constructed of a single piece of gold with a predominant center shaft having six branches, three on each side. A regular supply of oil fueled the lamps. Symbolically, the lamp represents the spiritual enlightenment that God gives His people through His revelation. David noted the link between light and life: "For with thee is the fountain of life: in thy light shall we see light" (Ps. 36:9). The New Testament suggests the same when it speaks of the light of the gospel (2 Cor. 4:4). If the light represents the gospel, the lampstand is a picture prophecy (type) of both Christ and the church, corporately and individually. The Lord Jesus identified Himself and believers as the light of the world (Matt. 5:14; John 8:12). That the seven churches in the book of the Revelation are designated as seven lampstands confirms the corporate relevance.

I would infer from the construction that the predominant center shaft specifically points to Christ, who, as the ideal Prophet, reveals God and truth. The branches with their lamps seemingly directing light to the center shaft picture the function of the church to bear witness to Christ, "the true Light, which lighteth every man that cometh into the world" (John 1:9). Indeed, the ministry of John the Baptist sums up the ministry of the church as a whole: "He was not that Light, but was sent to bear witness of that Light" (John 1:8; see also Isa. 60:1–3; 62:1–2; Matt. 5:14, 16). Furthermore, because the lampstand was a single piece of gold, the branches could not be separated from the center shaft. Just so are believers inseparably united to Christ. The lampstand by itself pictures some profound theology.

However, the distinctive components of Zechariah's vision suggest that the main point for Zerubbabel and us concerned the functioning of the lampstand and its supply of oil necessary for its functioning. This is why I've titled this section "Power for Service." Even in the lampstand in the tabernacle and temple, oil was the energy source. Not only was this actually necessary, but because oil was such a common symbol of the Holy Spirit in the Old Testament, it has spiritual implications as well. The Holy Spirit empowered Christ for His messianic mission; Christ had the Spirit without measure. The Holy Spirit not only dwells within believers, but He also empowers and enables believers every time they ask for His gracious power (Luke 11:13). The light cannot shine without the oil.

The distinctive components are the bowl on top of the lampstand, the seven pipes from the bowl to each of the lamps, and the two olive trees on either side with two troughs transferring oil from the trees directly to the bowl. In the tabernacle economy the continuity of the light depended on the people, who were to supply the olive oil, and on the ministry of the priests, who were to assure the lights were burning morning and evening (Ex. 27:20–21; 30:7–8). But in Zechariah's vision, there were no "middle men"; there was a constant, inexhaustible supply of oil directly from the source of the oil to the lamp. Translating the symbolism to reality means that there is an inexhaustible supply of the Holy Spirit available to God's servants to provide power to perform their service, their kingdom work.

That is what Zechariah saw, and the message of an inexhaustible supply of the Spirit's power is precisely the word Zerubbabel needed. Remember that as the civil authority, Zerubbabel was commissioned to oversee the rebuilding of the temple. But it was during his administration that the opposition from the outside, greater than Zerubbabel could resolve on his own, halted the project. This visionary word through Zechariah was right on point to help Zerubbabel accomplish his service, guaranteeing that the temple would stand again. Since Malachi would reveal that the Messiah was going to appear suddenly in the temple (Mal. 3:1), a standing temple was an essential step toward the fullness of time. This vision, therefore, of the Spirit's engagement and empowering was an important point in the progression of God's redemptive purpose and plan. The picture suggests three specific points with applications beyond Zerubbabel—a declaration, a promise, and an encouragement.

First, the divine *declaration* is that it is only by the power of the Holy Spirit that kingdom work can advance. The explanation from the interpreting angel has given classic expression to this truth: "Not by might, nor by power, but by my spirit, saith the LORD of hosts" (4:6). The word "might" literally has the idea of capacity and ranges in reference from notions of the valor of courage or the wealth of riches to virtue of character. But it also at times refers to an army. The notion of corporate or collective strength (such as that of an army) is likely in view here, particularly as it is paired with the word "power." This word, referring to ability or strength, applies regularly to individuals. Putting the two words together removes any chance for any human resource, whether personal charisma or collective organization, to be the effective agent in administering or accomplishing kingdom work. But what man or men are incapable of doing, the Spirit of the Lord can do. If anything is to be accomplished in the name of the Lord for the Lord's cause, the Lord Himself in the person of the Holy Spirit must operate and supply the power for service. Zerubbabel had seemingly found the end of the rope; he by this time knew that it would not be by might or power. Here is his word of hope: the work would progress by "my spirit, saith the LORD of hosts" (4:6).

The principle that was true then is just as true now. Yet many Christians and churches today attempt the work of God with human plans, innovative techniques, seminars for success, gimmicks, and promotions, with no thought of the Holy Spirit's empowering for service. Zechariah 4:6 needs to be the mantra for every Christian engaged in service to the Lord.

Second, the *promise* is that every obstacle will be removed and the work will be completed (4:7). When the Spirit works, there will be success; His power is irresistible. The obstacles are described in terms of a mountain that would appear to be impassable. Yet it will be flattened to become a plain, suited for unhindered travel. The work that had been stalled will be finished. The headstone, typically the topmost stone that marks the completion of a structure, will be fitted into its place. The shouts of double grace express both the jubilation over the completion and the desire for God's favor to rest upon the finished work. That the work will be completed will be irrefutable evidence of the Lord's working through the whole process (4:9). Hope fulfilled would be the rebuilt temple.

Third, the *encouragement* is not to be discouraged at what may seem to be a small and insignificant task. Asking the question, "Who hath despised the day of small things?" (4:10) presupposes that some were in fact despising or showing contempt or despite for the work. Remember that Haggai referred to those who had seen Solomon's temple and were put off by the lesser prospect of the second temple. The response to that notion was that faithfulness in serving the Lord is more important than the size of the work or the natural ability required for doing it. Even the smallest and most insignificant task done for the sake of the kingdom brings joy to the Lord. This more literal translation of verse 10 makes the point clearly: "Those seven, the eyes of the Lord which are roaming about the whole earth, will rejoice and see the plummet in the hand of Zerubbabel." The reference to the seven eyes of the Lord is a figurative way of expressing His omniscience; He sees and knows everything. Nothing escapes Him. The plummet was simply a line used to measure straightness. It does not take much skill to hold the plumb line, but when the plumb line was held in service to the Lord, God was pleased. That is amazing and encouraging, especially to so many believers who think they have nothing of value to offer.

This, indeed, should be reassuring to every Christian this side of Pentecost. The Spirit's empowering that Zerubbabel experienced, as the leader in the kingdom work, is now available to every believer, regardless of what the sphere of service may be. There is no work so small or insignificant that we should attempt it in our own strength; there is no work so small or insignificant that God will not see and rejoice over it when done for Him.

The point of the vision is clear: there is power for service. But after the vision and its explanation, Zechariah still had a question for the interpreting angel regarding the identity of the two olive trees. The answer does not affect the point of the picture, but it does draw a line to Christ. It is always good to follow that line wherever the Old Testament draws it. The angel, although a bit shocked that Zechariah does not know (4:13), identifies the two trees as "the two anointed ones, that stand by the Lord of the whole earth" (4:14). At first, the answer doesn't appear to help much, but further reflection suggests some significant trinitarian theology. Literally it says "the two sons of oil," suggesting the origin of the oil that flows to the lampstand. Typically, this points to the true son of oil, or anointed Messiah, who unites in one person each of the mediatorial offices, two of which are in view in Zerubbabel and Joshua, the central figures in visions 4 and 5. So the two trees together represent Christ. Christ, then, is standing next to Jehovah; the oil, or Holy Spirit, is flowing from Christ. Each of the persons of the Holy Trinity is in view. The picture, in essence, portrays the truth expressed in the Athanasian Creed: "The Holy Spirit is of the Father and of the Son; neither made, nor created, nor begotten, but proceeding."

Vision 6: Justice for Sinners

The principal picture of the sixth vision is a flying scroll measuring twenty by ten cubits (5:1–4). That converts to about thirty by fifteen feet; it is a big scroll. Relevant to the point of the vision is that those are the dimensions of the Holy Place in the tabernacle as traditionally understood by calculating the sizes of boards described in Exodus 26. To see the significance, we need to get right to the point, which is precisely where the interpreting angel took Zechariah after he described what he saw. The interpreter identified the scroll as "the curse that goeth forth over the face of the whole earth" (5:3). Something was written on the scroll that exposed thieves and perjurers, cutting them off or purging them out, and sentenced them to destruction even from

the apparent safety of their own houses (5:3–4). Being consumed (5:4) has the idea of finishing or bringing to an end;
the execution of justice will be thorough and irreversible.
Thus explained Zechariah's tutor.

Employing the analogy of Scripture (using Scripture
to interpret Scripture) enables us to be even more specific. Moses said, "Cursed be he that confirmeth not all
the words of this law to do them" (Deut. 27:26). What was
true in the Old Testament remains true in the New as Paul
makes clear by repeating Moses' words in Galatians 3:10
and by explaining in Romans 4:15 that "where no law is,
there is no transgression." All this points to the conclusion
that what Zechariah saw flying all over was the standard
of God's righteous and moral law, the standard by which
all will be judged without discrimination. The scroll found
transgressors, so it must be the law. The logic is clear
enough. Perhaps, then, the scroll's dimensions equaling the
Holy Place suggest the sanctuary standards, the divinely
sacred rule of holiness by which sinners will be exposed,
evaluated, and executed.

The main point is that God will deal with individual
sinners; justice will be served. The fact that only thieves
and liars are mentioned does not exclude or exempt other
transgressors from receiving justice. On the one hand,
mentioning two categories of sinners indicates how thoroughly and specifically the law identifies sinners. None
can escape. On the other hand, mentioning only a part is
a literary device (brachylogy) used to designate totality. If
every conceivable kind of sinner or sin were named, the
list would be endless. The partial list makes the point that

every individual will be judged according to the strict standard of righteousness. The flying scroll, representing God's inflexible and unchanging laws, is like a military drone, an eye in the sky, on a mission to discover the enemy's presence and to detect his movements and behavior. So all the world is accountable to God, liable to the just penalty of the broken law, and incapable of escaping the just consequences. It is good to remember that God is no respecter of persons and that none are exempt from His righteous judgment. To be outside of Christ is to be left with no defense against the curse.

Even a message of judgment serves a redemptive purpose by warning against the danger of rejecting the hope that is found in Christ. Nothing is more fearful than the prospect of God's justice—getting what we deserve. Our hope is that Christ came to take what we deserve.

Vision 7: Triumph over Evil

Whereas the vision of the flying scroll addressed God's dealing with individual sinners, the vision of the woman in the ephah addresses how God will deal with the principle of sin itself (5:5–11). He will triumph over all evil. The day is coming when every vestige of sin will be gone. The day is coming when there will be a complete reversal of the curse and a perfect environment for God's people to live in perfect communion and enjoyment of Him. There will be no more obstacles to His glory or hindrances to the holiness of His people. Wickedness will never tempt or trouble again. The prospect of this hope is so wonderfully glorious I've made the point before looking at the picture. So now that we know what the vision is about, let's look at the picture.

The principal parts of the vision are the woman in the ephah, the two women with stork-like wings, and Shinar. Zechariah first sees an ephah whose "resemblance" is "through all the earth" (5:6). An ephah was a dry measure, the largest in everyday common use and roughly equivalent to a bushel basket. The exact proportions are not as significant as the basket's function of carrying a load. It was a receptacle for collecting, transporting, and deposing. "Resemblance" is literally "their eye" and refers to its appearance throughout the land. Surprisingly, when the lid (the talent of lead, referring to a circular disk) was removed, a single woman was sitting, having been stuffed into the basket (5:7).

At this point the interpreting angel begins to explain what the prophet was seeing. He identifies the woman as wickedness (5:8) that was put inside the basket, which was then covered with the lid (the weight of lead on the basket's mouth or opening). The identity of the woman is a crucial component in the vision. That wickedness is a woman is the convention of Hebrew grammar, not a comment on womanhood. Hebrew has only two genders, masculine and feminine. Gender is a matter of grammar and not a reflection of reality. I often tell my students that grammar and reality are not the same, and that certainly applies to gender. The feminine gender often personifies abstract ideas, whether good or bad, vice or virtue (see the personification of wisdom in Proverbs 1, 8, and 9). The point is not that a woman is contained, but that wickedness is. Wickedness is trapped in such a way that it cannot escape.

Adding to the strangeness of the sight are two women who appear with stork-like wings that lift the basket and transport it to Shinar and put it in its own place (5:9–11). Storks are known for the strength of their wings, which here enable these two women to lift the basket high and carry it far away. The women are not identified specifically but represent the means by which wickedness is going to be removed. Shinar is an old name for Babylon, a place symbolic of wickedness, going all the way back to Genesis 10:10 and 11:2. Significantly, this confined wickedness will be imprisoned in a house, implying a fixed and permanent residence. The influence of wickedness will be removed once for all. God is triumphant; this is a vision of the manifestation of His ultimate and final victory over evil. This hope fulfilled is the eternal reign of righteousness without any threat of rebellion.

Vision 8: Final Victory

The final vision brings us back full circle to the issue in the first. In the first vision, the horses, representing the angelic agents of divine providence, reported that the nations that had afflicted Judah remained at rest in peace and quiet. That report caused the Angel of the Lord (the preincarnate Christ) to pray for God to show mercy to His people by executing vengeance on the enemies (1:12–15). In the last vision, the horses report that vengeance has indeed been executed (6:8). Christ's prayer is answered, and this last vision symbolically details that answer. This vision concerns

the final defeat of Judah's enemies, the anticipated fulfillment of which was a motivating hope for those struggling
to advance the kingdom by their rebuilding the temple in
the face of opposition.

The principal symbolism in the final vision centers on
the horses in the chariots and their activity (6:1–8). Zechariah first sees four chariots between two brass or, more
precisely, bronze mountains. Since bronze is often associated with and symbolic of judgment, the idea is that these
chariots are stationed on the ready to execute a work of
judgment. Although Joel 3:16 reveals that in divine judgment God will roar from Mount Zion and Zechariah 14:4
links judgment to the Mount of Olives, the identification of
the mountains in this vision is not germane to the picture;
just see them as representing the place of judgment. The
translation "chariot" is a bit misleading given our common
notion of a chariot as a combat vehicle carrying warriors
with their weapons. The word here refers to war wagons
used more for transporting supplies than for engaging in
the fray. This explains why the text specifically says that the
multicolored horses were in the wagons, not pulling them.
The horses were cargo in the wagons parked and ready to
be deployed from judgment headquarters.

Interestingly, the horses were segregated in the four
wagons according to their colors except in the fourth: red in
the first, black in the second, white in the third, but grisled
and bay horses in the fourth. "Grisled" refers to those that
were piebald or dappled. The word translated "bay" is not
a color, but refers rather to their being strong. The interpretation question is whether the colors are integral to

the message or just incidental. Red may symbolize war; white, victory; black, death; and piebald a combination of war and victory. But having said that, I am only guessing. Unlike the horses in John's apocalyptic vision in Revelation 6 whose colors are contextually defined, this text does not seem to link any particular activity to the color. I won't be dogmatic, but it is my opinion that in both of Zechariah's visions involving multicolored horses (the first and last), the colors are incidental other than expressing that God has multiple servants at His command and disposal to accomplish His purpose.

This is confirmed when the interpreting angel identifies who the horses are and what their commission is. He tells Zechariah, "These are the four spirits of the heavens, which go forth from standing before the Lord of all the earth" (6:5). So as in the first vision, the horses represent God's angels, ministering spirits who are agents of His providence (see Ps. 104:4; Heb. 1:14). Significantly, they are here "standing before the LORD of all the earth," ready to do His bidding. "Lord" here is the word for master or owner and conveys God's absolute authority over all.

Verses 6 and 7 detail their commission. The black horses go north, and the white horses follow them. The piebald horses head south, and the strong horses (bay) go everywhere. Each group receives the same orders; they are just deployed in service to different places. The north and south are singled out because of their particular relationships to Judah. The south most likely represents Egypt and the north represents Babylon, the principal enemy at this time and the primary focus of attention in the vision.

But thanks to the strong horses, every part of the earth is covered. Interestingly, the red horses go nowhere; they are kept in reserve, standing by the Lord ready to serve whenever He would order. All this suggests that God's resources are unlimited to accomplish His purposes. His power and authority are infinite.

Ironically, the horse report in the first vision disclosed that the nations hostile to God's people were at rest, living in peace and quiet (1:11). That report led to God's expressed displeasure "with the heathen that are at ease" (1:15) and to His promise to return to "Jerusalem with mercies" (1:16). In this last vision, the report about the north country (Babylon) has brought rest to the Lord: "Behold, these that go toward the north country have quieted my spirit in the north country" (6:8). God's anger has ceased; His displeasure has been appeased. When this hope would be fulfilled, all would be well. Regardless of how hostile worldly enemies may be, God has the final victory.

The war wagons and angelic forces at God's command in Zechariah's day are still operative as God's providence rules and subdues all forces hostile to the advance of His kingdom. The God of then is the God of now. We cannot see what is happening in the spiritual realm, but that does not mean that nothing is happening. Beyond our sight God is controlling everything to the certain accomplishment of His redemptive plan. Things had to be done in Zechariah's day for the preparation of the incarnation; things are being done in our day leading to the second coming. We may not understand what is happening at any given time, but faith rests in God's promise.

Reflecting on Zechariah's great message of hope justifies labeling him as the idealist. What God has in store for His people is beyond complete comprehension. If the certain fulfillment of hope was not founded firmly on God's word and power and focused squarely on His Christ, it would be nothing but utopian idealism, a pie-in-the-sky dream. But Zechariah's message makes clear at every juncture that God is working with unrelenting resolve and irresistible power to accomplish every promise He has made and every plan He has revealed. Zechariah's congregation lived in the reality of that hope and did their part in advancing the kingdom as they finished the work of rebuilding the temple. God is the same now as He was then, and His purpose and plan for complete and full redemption have not changed. Let us, therefore, live in the reality of the certain hope.

QUESTIONS

This is a longer chapter covering a big portion of Zechariah, so there are a few more questions to consider.

1. God spoke to Zechariah through visions. From your knowledge of the Bible, what other examples of visions can you identify?

2. Using a concordance, identify other occasions where the Angel of the Lord appeared. Look at the contexts and determine the purpose of His appearing.

3. In what way is the Angel of the Lord evidence of the Trinity?

4. Why was Zechariah's vision of the Angel of the Lord not technically a christophany?

5. Explain how Ephesians 3:20 sums up Zechariah 2. Meditate on the personal significance of this truth.

6. Why is it hard to believe as much and as fervently as we should? Regarding this problem, what should be our prayer?

7. What was the twofold purpose of walls that would make them unnecessary? How does that twofold purpose apply personally?

8. Where and how can we see the Trinity in Zechariah 2?

9. Why is Babylon referred to as north when it is geographically east?

10. Why is it important for believers to separate from the world?

11. Put yourself in Joshua's place in the courtroom and reflect on the wonder of the gospel of grace.

12. What is the difference between a symbol and a type?

13. What is the difference between the indwelling of the Holy Spirit and the empowering of the Holy Spirit?

14. What kind of "plumb-line" jobs can you do in the service of God's kingdom?

15. How does the vision of the flying scroll illustrate the unity of the Ten Commandments?

—PART 4—

Malachi: The Logician

Facts about Malachi

Apart from his name, we know nothing about Malachi. In fact, some don't even think we know that much. *Malachi* means "my messenger," and is exactly the same form that occurs in 3:1 where the Lord says, "I will send my messenger." Consequently, some think that "Malachi," or "my messenger," in 1:1 is simply a title designating an otherwise anonymous prophet. There is a long history of speculation regarding the identity of the author. The Septuagint, the Greek translation of the Hebrew Scriptures, did not recognize *Malachi* to be a proper name and so translated it as "his messenger or angel" rather than transliterating it, which was the normal practice for names. The translator, most likely, changed the number of the pronoun from the first person (my) to the third person (his) because the "my" would have no antecedent or referent in the rest of the verse. That fact, by the way, lends grammatical support to taking Malachi as a proper name. The Aramaic Targum, the Aramaic translation of the Hebrew Scriptures with incorporated commentary, identifies the author of the prophecy as Ezra. On the other hand, the Vulgate, the Latin version of the Bible, interprets Malachi as a proper name, as does the AD second century uninspired and noncanonical book of 2 Esdras that links Malachi to Haggai and Zechariah (2 Esd.1:40). This is interesting but ultimately without consequence in terms of the book's authority and integrity.

Some critical scholars, however, regard Malachi as the third in a series of anonymous oracles, each beginning with the statement "the burden of the word of the LORD" (1:1; see also Zech. 9:1; 12:1). Not only does this affect the understanding of Malachi, it also seriously undermines the integrity and unity of Zechariah by postulating the existence of a Deutero-Zechariah (9–11) and a Trito-Zechariah (12–14), neither of which were from Zechariah but were incorrectly appended to his book. Critics can't agree whether these supposed appendixes to Zechariah are preexilic (making them really early) or post-Alexandrian (making them really late); they just seem to be certain that the two sections could not be from Zechariah. The third-burden message (Malachi) remained, for whatever reason, independent.

Traditionally, most conservatives regard Malachi as the personal name of the prophet who is the sole author of the book, and that is my position. The grammar of 1:1 leads to this conclusion: the absence of any antecedent to the pronoun "my" and the fact that the expression "by the hand of" is usually followed by a proper name in the Hebrew, but simply translated "by" in the King James Version. However, since the purpose of this study is to focus on the prophet's message and not the evaluation or refutation of critical notions, I am going to leave it at that.

The Man

Malachi was the last named prophet before the next named messenger, John the Baptist, would appear to prepare the way for the ideal and final Messenger, Jesus Himself. Malachi's prophetic message is, therefore, the last of the next-to-last words. Although Malachi says nothing about himself and does not date his prophecy as explicitly as Haggai and Zechariah do, he does give sufficient clues to identify the date and thus the historical setting of his ministry. Knowing something about the historical context is always crucial for the interpretative process.

Most obvious is that his ministry was after the completion of the temple (516 BC) since he addresses serious abuses and breaches of Mosaic protocol. The degeneration of worship practices was probably gradual, so his preaching would have been some time after that momentous day when the temple doors were opened for the renewal of the ceremonies. Other issues and circumstances suggest some link to the time of Nehemiah, such as corruption in the priesthood (Mal. 1:6–2:9; Neh. 13:7–9); violations of the Sabbath (Mal. 2:8–9; Neh. 13:15–22); mixed-faith marriages (Mal. 2:11–15; Neh. 13:23–27); and ignoring the tithe (Mal. 3:8–10; Neh. 12:44; 13:5, 10). Although critics generally date their unnamed prophet to the first half of the fifth century BC, it is more likely that Malachi prophesied a bit later, around 435 BC, and thus was a contemporary with Nehemiah, who first returned to Palestine in 445 BC. The date 435 BC would put Malachi's ministry between the two governorships of Nehemiah in Palestine (read Nehemiah for the events of his career). Almost one hundred years after

Haggai and Zechariah started their ministries (520 BC), Malachi had a new message, a new burden, from the Lord. The stage was set. We must understand Malachi in the light of what came before him.

By proclaiming the glorious prospects of the messianic age, Haggai and Zechariah inspired the discouraged returnees from Babylon to be diligent in their service to the Lord and to complete the reconstruction of the fallen temple. When they preached, the nation was still under foreign domination, Jerusalem lay in ruins, and David's throne was empty. Yet the prophetic message of peace and prosperity and the promise of divine presence was enough to encourage the people for the task at hand. The temple was soon completed. The only thing missing was the experience of the greater glory that Haggai predicted would fill the second temple. Now almost one hundred years passed without the realization of the expected promises. The nation remained subject to the same foreign power (although now under Artaxerxes instead of Darius), and there was no immediate prospect for a king on David's throne. The people were not experiencing the blessings that they assumed God had promised and that they thought they most certainly deserved. Believing that they had done everything God had demanded, they grew increasingly impatient with the divine delays. Because God did not act according to their agenda or schedule, they began to doubt His word and His ability to keep His promise. God raised up Malachi to put things in the right perspective.

It is not unusual for God's people to struggle as they seek resolution to the tension between what they believe and what they experience. The Scripture records many examples of this faith/experience conflict, as do our personal diaries. As examples, Job, Jeremiah, Asaph, and Habakkuk puzzled over what appeared to be anomalies of providence; indeed, every believer has too. But the people to whom Malachi unburdened himself were guilty of more than the normal struggles of faith. These people had developed serious misconceptions of God and of the nature of true, spiritual worship. God was someone who owed them things, and religion was a means of manipulating God for a better life. The people were obsessed with life "here and now" with no concern for the more important issues of "there and then." Malachi had a message that went right to the point.

The Message

Malachi's message was squarely targeted against the improper and insincere religion that characterized his day. His aim was to awaken a people whose religious cynicism and skepticism of God's promises led to careless and dead worship and to renew hope and revive true religion in view of the certainty of God's purpose. Wrong thinking about God and wrong worship of God go together. So Malachi's exposing and rebuking insincere worship had to include his correcting false notions about God. Consequently, his prophecy takes on the traits of a theodicy, that which is a defense of God's goodness and justice. In his inspired theodicy, Malachi made it unmistakably clear with irrefutable logic that the blame for any lack of blessing did not rest on God's unfaithfulness or injustice but on the spiritual deadness and the failure of the nation to behave according to the demands of grace.

The details of Malachi's message will follow, but there are some general themes to keep in focus as the specifics come to view. The covenant between God and Israel is at the foundation of Malachi's theodicean argument. A proper understanding and application of covenant theology would be the corrective against the false notions and bad practices that Malachi had to confront. Understanding the covenant would preclude any thought of God's being unfaithful and would prevent any self-justification. Although the people accused God of reneging on His promises and becoming distant, Malachi presented overwhelming evidence of God's nearness and faithfulness both to His promises and to Himself. The prevalence of the covenant name Jehovah, especially compounded with "hosts," reinforces the special dealings of God with Israel. In this short book consisting of only fifty-five verses, the title "Jehovah of Hosts" occurs almost twenty-five times. This lofty title identifies God as the commander in chief with all power and authority and with all resources at His disposal to accomplish His purpose. Any lack of blessing was not due to His purpose or inability. In fact, His being the covenant-keeping Jehovah was the only explanation for the nation's existence: "For I am the LORD, I change not; therefore ye sons of Jacob are not consumed" (3:6). In addition to the frequent use of the covenant name, the Lord addresses the people directly with first-person personal pronouns over sixty times. There can be no doubt that the Lord is a personal God who had entered into a special covenant relationship with these people. He was not at all distant from them, as they had surmised.

In keeping with the covenant foundation of his message, Malachi highlights as well the demands of the gracious covenant on the people. God was faithful to the covenant; the expectation was that the people would be faithful too. Throughout the prophecy, Malachi exposes the flagrant disregard and disobedience of their covenant obligations. They were guilty of dishonoring God (1:6); offering unlawful sacrifices (1:13); and sorcery, adultery, perjury (3:5), and treachery against each other, which Malachi directly identified as a profaning of the covenant (2:10), and the list goes on. The evidence is overwhelming that the state of affairs of the nation was not due to God's failure to fulfill His promises but to the nation's disloyalty and disobedience. In fact, the dismal state of the nation was the consequence of God's executing the necessary and well-publicized curses for covenant transgression (see especially Leviticus 26; Deuteronomy 28). It is not surprising that Malachi, in true prophetic tradition, so closely explains their condition in the light of Mosaic covenant theology: "Remember ye the law of Moses my servant, which I commanded unto him in Horeb for all Israel, with statutes and judgments" (4:4). Malachi is just one more in the long line of reformation prophets.

Happily, Malachi's message is not without hope, and it is a hope that centers on Christ. In fear-producing sobriety, he ends his message with the threat of curse and judgment in 4:6: "lest I come and smite the earth with a curse." Yet before the execution of that "great and dreadful day of the

LORD" (4:5), there is the prospect and hope of healing. The answer to the curse is developed in terms of a coming Messenger of the covenant who will be preceded by a messenger, a forerunner in the spirit of Elijah (3:1; 4:5). This final Messenger is the "Sun of righteousness," who will "arise with healing in his wings" (4:2). Undoubtedly, this would have been the portion of Malachi that the resurrected Lord Jesus explained to the two disciples on the road to Emmaus when, beginning with Moses and all the prophets, He expounded "in all the scriptures the things concerning himself" (Luke 24:27). The answer to the deadness and dearth of Malachi's day was Christ and the gospel. That is not surprising since that is the answer to the issues of every day.

The Method

Malachi's method of presenting his message is why I've characterized him as the logician. His methodology is on the surface of his prophecy, and virtually anything ever written about Malachi or preached from it has recognized the obvious structure. In an artful, unrelenting, irrefutable dialectic, Malachi exposed the worthless religion and arrogant self-perspective of the people who thought more of themselves than of God. The term *dialectic* refers to the art of investigating or discussing some issue. Malachi's logic is also frequently described as a *disputation*, referring to a formal, academic-like debate. His procedure was impeccable. The format is easily recognized and is the basis for most outlines of the book. It begins with a proposition or assertion of fact that is followed by a question expressing a denial of the proposition that is then followed by undeniable proof of the proposition. Significantly, the denial of the proposition reveals one of the evidences of heartless, dead religion. Dead religion tends to breed a carnal security, convincing the practitioner that all is well with God when in reality it is not well at all.

There are six of these disputation formulas that suggest the following outline, which will provide the overall structure for my survey of the book's message.

    I. Introduction (1:1)
    II. Insensitivity to Grace (1:2–5)
    III. Insincere Worship (1:6–2:9)
    IV. Instability in Families (2:10–16)
    V. Inaccurate Views of God (2:17–3:7)
    VI. Insufficient Giving (3:8–12)
    VII. Improper Motives for Service (3:13–4:3)
    VIII. Conclusion (4:4–6)

Although written over twenty-four hundred years ago, Malachi's message is tragically relevant for today. Although the mechanics of worship may be different, the same mercantile, self-focused religion lives on. A perfunctory, dead, external, formalistic religion has never satisfied God. Malachi's analysis of the dead religion of his day is a casebook for God's modern-day messengers who must expose the same kind of spiritual death, proclaim the same warning, and prescribe the same remedy.

Malachi argues as a brilliant prosecutor and logician, but his analysis of formalistic and dead religion reminds me of an autopsy. The purpose of an autopsy is to discover the cause of death by examining the corpse for signs of decay and malfunction. Often discovering the cause of death in one person leads to the preserving of life in many others. So I will look at Malachi not so much as a lawyer but as a theological pathologist who meticulously examines, exposes, and identifies the causes and signs of dead religion and spiritual decay. In so doing, I will present his dialectic in terms of six cutting propositions that penetrate to the core issues that marked Israel's religion. Discovering what killed their religion will help preserve the religion of others. We can do this under three broad heads: the autopsy of dead religion, the answer to dead religion, and the antithesis to dead religion.

QUESTIONS

1. The faith/experience conflict was at the core of the problem Malachi had to confront. Most likely you have struggled with this tension as well. Why is this a common problem, and how should we deal with it?

2. What is a theodicy? Note this could apply to the book of Job as well. As you think about Job, why could this designation apply? (This is just something to think about on your own; the answer is not in the chapter.)

3. Why and how is the covenant such an important component in Malachi's argument?

4. What evidence is there that Malachi is a "reformation" prophet?

16

The Autopsy of Dead Religion

Although Malachi's process in addressing the problems of his nation betrays the logic of the lawyer, the subject of his analysis (dead religion) hints at the work of a pathologist performing an autopsy. So putting this twist on Malachi's disputation, I want to observe his procedure and the precision with which he cuts to the very core of the spiritual corpse. Admittedly, the analogy will fall apart in places, but it will nonetheless identify the salient points of the message. As in any autopsy, some gruesome and gross things will be exposed, but dead and formalistic ritual is a disgusting thing to the Lord. It is not my purpose or plan to comment on everything Malachi puts on the table, but I do want to give a synopsis of his autopsy report of dead religion. With six well-placed incisions, Malachi identified the fatal symptoms.

Incision 1: Insensitivity to Grace

I don't know where physical autopsies begin, but spiritual autopsies begin with the heart. The first incision revealed insensitivity to grace (1:2–5). This examination uncovers the fact of grace, its denial, and its evidence. Malachi's first

pronouncement was a simple, yet profound declaration of
divine love: "I have loved you, saith the LORD" (1:2). The
word "love" is the principal Old Testament word to designate God's willful, sovereign, and gracious love, the reason
and motive for which is within God and not in what is
loved. Moses gave the only explanation that accounts for
divine love when he said that God loved His people because
He loved them (Deut. 7:7–8). To be loved by God is to be
favored with grace. The fact of grace is wonderfully amazing.

Pathologists performing autopsies "listen" to the corpse
to learn what it might "say" to give some clue as to the
cause of death. So, cutting to the heart of Malachi's patient
exposed an important clue. The first and fundamental
evidence of spiritual trouble was the denial of that love:
"Wherein hast thou loved us?" (1:2). Like a selfish child
who cries "Nobody loves me" when he does not get his own
way, Israel had interpreted their circumstances as evidence
that God did not love them. Because they were not experiencing the material blessing they thought they deserved,
they denied the reality of the freely declared love of God.

Malachi proved God's love in terms of unmerited election and unfailing preservation (1:2–5). The evidence of
grace was overwhelming, which only intensifies the hard-
ness, coldness, and insensitivity of the heart. The contrast
between Jacob and Esau highlights the absolute sovereignty
of divine love and grace (see Rom. 9:10–13). God's loving
Jacob and hating Esau were not petty emotional displays
earned by the behavior of Jacob and the misbehavior of
Esau or their descendants. Rather, loving and hating were
issues of deliberate divine choice. God accepted Jacob and

rejected Esau. No reason for the choice of Jacob is given; the choice is explicable only in terms of grace. There really was nothing likable, let alone lovable, about Jacob. He was without any virtue or merit. God's loving and choosing him instead of Esau was purely an expression of divine favor displayed altruistically to one who deserved no favor. Whereas Esau received what he deserved, Jacob did not. Esau's descendants, the Edomites, were the objects of God's indignation (1:4). In contrast, the Lord would be great in Israel (1:5).

For Israel to doubt God's love in the light of election and preservation was the height of ingratitude. Sensitivity to grace, on the other hand, always fosters thanksgiving and the realization that God's love is not to be measured by things but by the reality of a personal, intimate relationship with the Lord Himself. Religion will thrive and live well when and if God's people are overwhelmed with the amazing and wondrous grace of God.

Incision 2: Insincere Worship

The second incision revealed insincere worship (1:6–2:9). In 1:6–7 Malachi made two general accusations against the priests: that they were despising God's name and that they were polluting the bread on the altar. They, of course, denied the charges, and then Malachi proved the accusations and issued a stern warning. Although Malachi directed the charges against the priests, the application extended to the nation as a whole since priests, by definition, were the representatives of the people. As a rule, the spiritual state of the laity will not be better than that of the clergy (cf. Hos. 4:9). Although the priests were ordained to teach God's law by word and by example (2:6–7), they in practice "caused many to stumble at the law" (2:8). They seemed more concerned with pleasing the people than with pleasing God. They fostered an easy, insincere religion that was full of ritual and empty of spirit and truth. Malachi's twofold accusation suggests two distinctives of insincere worship.

First, insincere worship reveals irreverence toward God. True, spiritual worship is theocentric, evincing a proper knowledge and acknowledgment of God. In Malachi 1, the Lord of Hosts identified Himself as a father, a master, and a great king, whose name is worthy of fear (vv. 6, 14). Each of these titles, including the Lord of Hosts, focuses on God's eminent position, authority, honor, and power. Such a God deserves all the reverence, respect, and awe that the creature can give, and all that the creature can possibly give is infinitely insufficient to esteem Him for all His infinite worth. Notwithstanding the Lord's infinite greatness and innate honor, the priests despised His name (1:6). The word "despise" means "to think lightly of" or "to make light of" and "name" refers to the totality of God's person and perfection. It is a significant contrast to the word translated "honor" in 1:6 and "glory" in 2:2, which involves the idea of weight or heaviness. Whereas God in the totality of His being and perfections deserved to be regarded as heavy, they regarded Him as light. A light regard for God is never conducive to spiritual worship. Significantly, the key words for worship in both the Old and New Testaments suggest the idea of bowing down before the Lord. True worship cannot exist until man sees himself as little and God as big. Malachi's generation was more concerned with self-issues than with God's glory. They regarded their own concerns to be weightier than the Lord, and that affected their religious behavior. Tragically, many modern church services display the same light regard for God. Worship services have given way to entertainment hours and testimony times drawing attention to man's sacrificial accomplishments for God rather than directing hearts to bow before the holy person of the Lord.

Second, insincere worship expresses itself in empty ritual: a form of worship without the reality of truly seeking the Lord. Malachi accused the priests of offering polluted bread on the altar (1:7). The word "polluted" designates something that is ceremonially impure; it is unfit for worship. It may be something acceptable in other contexts, but it is inappropriate for the place of worship. They were guilty of regarding the holy place as a common place. Any offering was good enough for God, even if it was blind, sick, lame, or mauled (1:7–13). Not only did this express a "cheap religion," it also undermined the gospel message that the sacrifices were ordained to picture—the perfect righteousness of Christ as the only acceptable sacrifice for sin. Carelessly, thoughtlessly, and heartlessly, they went through the motions of worship, assuming God would be satisfied with whatever trinket they threw His way. The whole routine had become a nuisance (1:13) as they evidenced a "here-we-go-again" attitude. The Lord made it clear that He was not satisfied and would not accept their offerings (1:13). He cursed any who would treat Him with such contempt

(1:14). He particularly held the priests responsible, cursing them for disobedience (2:1–2), rebuking their descendants (2:3), and bringing them to shame (2:3, 9). God's spreading the dung on their faces was symbolic of His disgust over their offensive offerings.

The situation in modern Christianity is no better. On the one hand, many are bringing unfit and inappropriate things into the place of worship. "Seeker-sensitive" services are flexibly designed to eliminate religious shock by infusing cultural norms with a bit of gospel. Worship as entertainment prevails over worship as service rendered to God. The whole controversy about worship style has degenerated into arguments based on personal preferences rather than on scriptural principles. On the other hand, many regard worship as mere duty, a necessary nuisance. With trinkets of church attendance and formalistic and empty routine, they salve the conscience, believing that God will be satisfied with whatever takes place inside church walls. Dead religion exists in churches where people sway and run the aisles as easily as in churches that follow a strict and even Reformed liturgy. Malachi's message sounds the warning clearly that God will never be satisfied with thoughtless, heartless religion regardless of the form it takes, whether traditional or contemporary. Form of worship is important, but heart in worship is crucial.

Incision 3: Instability of Families

The third incision revealed unfaithfulness in human relationships (2:10–16). Loose worship and loose social morality always go together; carelessness about God affects everything. This section contains some of the most challenging points of Hebrew grammar and interpretation in the book, yet some of the most important and practical of truths. Notwithstanding some of the intricate details, the main message is clear enough. The section begins with the declared fact of God's authority and ownership: He is the Father who is worthy of honor and obedience, and the Creator who has exclusive rights of ownership and governance (2:10). Given who He is, the nation's behavior was contrary to expectation and incongruous. They behaved "treacherously," a word designating unfaithfulness and covenant violation, usually against the marriage bond. In 2:11 the prophet took the scalpel and sliced them open, exposing the fatal infection. The deadly disease was their corrupting the covenant with God by intermarrying with the heathen ("the daughter of a strange [foreign] god"). Intermarriage with unbelievers was wrong because God had chosen Israel to be a separated people. They were repudiating God's purpose for them by behaving like the world (see Deut. 7:2–4). The consequences were inescapable, as both the master and the scholar (an idiom expressing inclusiveness) would be cut off regardless of the extremes of the unacceptable religious rigmarole they employed (2:12–13).

As Malachi cut a little deeper, he uncovered the evidence to support the initial diagnosis (2:14–16). Malachi showed how sinful this behavior was in three ways. First, men had broken faith with their first wives, violating their marriage contracts. He reminded them that when they acted unfaithfully in violating the covenant with their wives, they sinned against God. God had witnessed their covenant vows, and He expected them to fulfill them (2:14). Second, he put before them one of the ideals of marriage that God intended. God had made husband and wife one (see Gen. 2:24), and no one who has a portion of the spirit will violate that union. A key purpose of the union is the production of a godly seed. It is the special design of the covenant family to be a breeding ground for the church. Therefore, to violate this sacred union would be a tragedy. Third, he declared that God hated divorce (putting away). God had made woman to be the perfect complement for man, pairing them together and uniting them into one flesh. Divorce breaks the bond that God had sealed.

It is not without significance that in Malachi's day, as in ours, the home was a battleground rather than heaven on earth (Deut. 11:21). The breakup of homes is irrefutable evidence that many hearts are not right with the Lord. The home is always the test of how real religion is. Indeed, religion is no more real than it is in the home. Discord in the home is evidence of dead, inactive religion in most cases. Godly homes make for godly churches.

Incision 4: Inaccurate Views of God

The fourth incision revealed misconceptions of God (2:17–3:7). Dead religion tends to base its definition of God on sight rather than on faith, on appearance rather than on reality. The apparent prosperity of the wicked contrasted with the apparent adversity of the righteous caused the self-righteous to question the justice of God (2:17). Because they were not enjoying the prosperity they thought they deserved, they concluded that God was not fair and that He was more pleased with sinners than saints. There is always a natural tendency to define fairness in terms of self. Dead, formal religion breeds a security and carnal confidence that will sooner find fault with God than with self. In a bold anthropopathism, God charged the nation with wearying Him with their words. They had made Him sick and tired by their constant complaining and selfish perspectives. Theologically, we know that God is a spirit without body parts or human passions or emotions (see Westminster Confession of Faith, 2.1). God is immutable and absolutely independent. He does not change and is unaffected in His internal being by anything external to Himself. So God's claim that He is weary provides a vivid image of how offensive their charges against Him were.

Faith knows that the prosperity of the wicked is only apparent and temporary (see Psalms 37, 49, and 73). It is foolish, therefore, to envy the wicked because they are under God's certain wrath and condemnation. Faith knows that this life, even at its worst, is the best it will ever be for the ungodly and that this life, even at its best, is the worst it will ever be for the godly. Living religion looks to eternity. But when all you can see is yourself, and self becomes the criterion for judging God, misconceptions are inevitable.

The rest of this section, beginning in chapter 3, details part of the solution or answer to dead religion. It is a great answer that brings us directly to Christ, but we will consider it in the next chapter.

Incision 5: Insufficient Giving

The fifth incision revealed the people's departure from God's ordinances evidenced in their failure to give to God the required tithes and offerings (3:7–12). This act of robbery was another evidence of dead, heartless religion. The tithe demonstrated recognition of God for His gracious supply of the bounty of life and thanksgiving for His goodness (cf. Lev. 27:30). Significantly, when the people had a heart for God, giving was abundant and natural (cf. Ex. 35:21, 29). But now, as another evidence of their spiritual malady, they withheld offerings from God and forfeited great blessings. Indeed, to bring the tithes into the storehouse (a chamber in the temple for depositing treasures) would generate such a return that they would be the "envy" of all the nations. That is the significance of the word "blessed" in verse 12. It is a descriptive word designating the fortunate condition observable to others, a desirable condition to be emulated. But don't misunderstand; God is no man's debtor. Giving to God is not to enrich Him, for the earth is His along with its fullness; God does not need anything. Nor is it a bargaining device or an investment token to get more from God; it is, rather, an expression of the enjoyment of the Lord Himself.

The requirement for tithes and offerings certainly refers to the liberal giving of material possessions, but it extends in principle to giving spiritual things as well. The more believers find satisfaction in the person of God rather than in possessions, the more freely they will give themselves and all they have to the Lord. Dead religion selfishly hoards; living religion selflessly gives.

The teaching of the Lord Jesus is to the point here as well when He instructed us to lay up our treasures in heaven instead of on the earth: "For where your treasure is, there will your heart be also" (Matt. 6:19–21). In true, biblical, living religion, everything keeps coming back to the heart.

Incision 6: Improper Motives for Service

The final incision in Malachi's autopsy of dead religion exposed improper motives (3:13–4:3). "Why" is as important as "what." In 3:13 the Lord accused the people of stout words. The word "stout" means hard, severe, or sharp. Their impudent, presumptuous words spewing out of a bad attitude had expressed violence toward God. In 3:14 the Lord identified precisely what the stout words were: "It is vain to serve God: and what profit is it that we have kept his ordinance?" This suggests that the people's motive for serving God was personal gain—religion for profit. Their calling service to God "vain" means that they saw it as useless, insubstantial, without value. That obedience was without profit means that they received no increase. The word "profit" is a weaver's term used of a piece of cloth that has been cut. The imagery is suggestive even if anachronistic: they had served the Lord, and they wanted their cut. When they saw no profit, they saw no reason for serving anymore. To serve God for profit is a faithless act, reflecting a materialistic spirit. Ironically, when blessing is defined in terms of material things that in turn become the goal of devotion and service, real blessing and reward from God will never be recognized.

Often this same deadness characterizes today's church. Full-time Christian service is often rejected because it does not pay. Those in such full-time service often moan over their sacrifice rather than rejoicing in their privilege. Some give to the Lord as if making an investment; they give to get. Wrong motives always kill good religion.

The rest of the section addresses part of the answer to dead religion and its antithesis by showing what living religion looks like and pointing to Messiah. That discussion is coming.

Malachi's autopsy has discovered the causes of the spiritual decay and dead religion that marked the people and explained the lack of spiritual blessing that blighted the land. Happily, there is a difference between Malachi's theological autopsy and those performed by coroners in the morgue. Physically dead corpses are doomed to the grave —at least until the resurrection day. But for Malachi's "corpse," there is hope. He is not done with his message. The book is not finished yet.

QUESTIONS

1. Why is the Hebrew word for *love* an appropriate term to refer to electing grace?

2. Why should reflection on God's love prevent coldness of heart? How often do you let your heart be overwhelmed with the thoughts of amazing grace?

3. In what ways do many modern church services resemble what was taking place in Malachi's day?

4. Why can it be said that religion is no more real than in the home? How real is your religion?

5. In what way does your giving reveal the condition of your heart before the Lord?

6. Why is materialism such an enemy to worship and service?

17

The Answer to Dead Religion

Sometimes it helps to put the bottom line right at the top. The bottom line is that the answer to every spiritual problem, including dead religion, is Christ. Significantly, Malachi gives that final answer in terms of the coming Day of the Lord. In 3:2 the prophet asked, "Who may abide the day of his coming?" In 4:1 he described the coming day as a time of burning in which neither root nor branch would survive and in 4:5 as a great and dreadful (fear-evoking) day. The Day of the Lord was a common prophetic theme. Beginning with Obadiah, the first of the writing prophets, until Malachi, the last of the Old Testament writing prophets, the announcement of the Day of the Lord, in part, delineated God's ultimate answer to sin. By simple definition, the Day of the Lord is the period in which God directly interrupts the affairs of time for either the judgment of the wicked (as in 4:1) or the blessing of the righteous (as in 4:2–3). Often the Day does both at the same time, for judgment on the wicked brings relief to the righteous. Simply defined, the Day of the Lord is when eternity breaks into time. Although there have been multiple days in which God has so intervened, there is yet one final, eschatological day that is certain to come and of which all the preceding days are in some way typical, that is, picture prophecies. Judgment, restoration, and messianic blessing are all common themes developed within the context of the Day of the Lord.

Although Malachi touches most of these common themes, at the heart of his message is the Messiah. In typical prophetic fashion (see 1 Peter 1:11), he fuses elements of the first and second advents of Christ, both of which constitute Days of the Lord. It was not his purpose to supply data for a strict eschatological chronology but rather to focus on the implications of Christ's coming—whether His first or second. For Malachi's argument, the certain *fact* of Messiah's coming was more crucial than the *when*. Indeed, the undefined *when* aided in the forceful application of the *fact*. Not knowing the *when* meant that one had to be ready for the *fact* that could happen at any time. From Malachi's day, it was going to be over four centuries before the first coming of Christ, and already it has been more than two millennia before the second coming, but the fact of both remains certain. Be ready!

Part of Malachi's purpose was to correct some tragic misunderstandings about Christ and His kingdom that characterized the thinking of his generation. Many had a messianic hope, but the Messiah of their anticipation was not the Christ of God; they were in for a surprise. Malachi's corrective echoed that of Amos, who three centuries earlier pronounced a woe on those who desired the Day of the Lord and who declared it to be a day of darkness rather than the light they anticipated (Amos 5:18–20). Practitioners of dead religion tend to assume that God is on their

side and that He will destroy their enemies, when in reality
they themselves stand in jeopardy of judgment. Similarly,
many today have notions of a Jesus who, in fact, is another
Jesus; they too will be surprised when the real Christ
appears. True worship, whether in the old or new dispensation, depends on the proper understanding of Jesus Christ.
Christianity has always been the one true religion.

Malachi's message is relatively short, so the messianic
texts are limited but pointed. In 4:2, he encourages those
who fear the Lord that the "Sun of righteousness" will
arise or shine "with healing in his wings" with the consequence that they will prosper (literally, they will frisk about
like young, strong bulls being fattened up in the stall) and
with bull-like strength will tread down the wicked, exercising dominion over them (4:3; see also Ps. 49:14). Although
interpreters disagree whether "Sun of righteousness" is a
messianic title, the evidence and attendant circumstances
of this Sun's shining ultimately are true only in terms of the
Messiah's work. It certainly parallels Zacharias's identification of the Lord, whose way his son John would prepare,
as "the dayspring from on high" who would "give light to
them that sit in darkness" (Luke 1:78–79). The word "dayspring" literally means "rising" and thus could well refer to
the sun's shining. That the Septuagint uses the same word
to translate the messianic title "Branch" in Jeremiah 23:5;
33:15; and Zechariah 3:8 may suggest that to be the basis
of Zacharias's statement. The messianic identification of the
Sun of righteousness does not ultimately depend on what
text Zacharias may have had in mind. For various reasons,
I'm happy enough to see it as a messianic title.

The key passage, however, that develops the messianic message is 3:1–6. It is the Lord's answer to the divinely wearying question, "Where is the God of justice?" (2:17, author's translation). The Lord's answer regarding His unchangeable justice was the coming Christ. I want to sum up the Lord's answer with four thoughts regarding Christ's certain coming. In a very real sense, Paul's "Maranatha," an Aramaic expression meaning "Our Lord comes" (1 Cor. 16:22), could be written over this section.

The Preparation for Christ's Coming

The Lord's answer to the question of where He was, which implied His inactivity (2:17), made it unmistakably clear that He was most active in the execution of His purpose and plan: "Behold, I will send my messenger" (3:1). A more literal translation underlines the pointed answer: "Here I am—I am about to send my messenger." The Hebrew construction is called a *futurum instans*, grammatical jargon to refer to an action that is impending or imminent, something that is certain to happen and could happen at any moment. God was setting something in motion that would progress without interruption until its accomplishment. A messenger to prepare the way of the Lord was coming. The image is of a forerunner who went in front of a dignitary to alert those along the travel route of the approaching king and to make sure the way was freed from obstacles that would hinder progress. This forerunner would conduct an Elijah-type ministry (3:1; 4:5–6). Although Malachi does not specifically identify this special messenger, the Gospels affirm that John the Baptist fulfilled this preparatory ministry for Christ's first advent (Matt. 11:14; 17:12; Mark 9:11–13; Luke 1:17). John's message focused on Christ and the necessity of repentance as the only way sinners could enjoy the presence of Christ. Such ministry is always a necessary prerequisite for preparing people to be ready for the coming of the Lord. This has significance in terms of both advents of Christ. Revelation 11 reveals two yet unidentifiable witnesses who will, in the spirit and power of Elijah and Moses, preach the gospel of repentance before Christ's glorious second coming.

The Promise of Christ's Coming

Malachi makes some significant statements in identifying the real Christ of God: who He is, where He is coming, and when. First, the coming Christ is God. This is both logically implicit and lexically explicit. Logically, 3:1 is the immediate answer to the final question of 2:17: "Where is the God of justice?" The Lord of Hosts basically declares that the God of justice is coming. The Lord of Hosts says, "I will send my messenger, and he will prepare the way before me." He follows that statement with "The Lord, whom ye seek, shall suddenly come to His temple, even the Messenger of the covenant.... Behold, he shall come" (author's translation). The shift between the first and third person in the declaration of the Lord of Hosts hints at the mystery of the Godhead. On the one hand, the Lord of Hosts says that a messenger will prepare the way before *me* (first person), and then, on the other hand, speaks of the Messenger of the covenant, who is the Lord, that *He* (third person) shall come. The coming One is both identified as, yet distinct from, the Lord of Hosts.

Lexically, the One coming is the Lord. The articular form "the Lord" occurs only eight times in the Old Testament and refers uniquely to deity. Like the more common form of the word without the article, it designates God as the master, owner, and controller of all. He cannot be manipulated or used. What a corrective to Israel's theology this was! It is clear from their accusation that implies God's injustice that they defined justice in terms of what was beneficial to them. So with a bit of perspicacious sarcasm, the prophet indicated that the Lord whom they were fervently seeking and delighting in (3:1) was not God's Christ. The real Christ was not what they conceived; they were in for a surprise. Whereas they wanted a savior that they could manipulate for personal advantage and who would deliver them from their troubles, the real Christ was the sovereign Lord who rules but is not ruled. Unless they were truly seeking and hoping for the real Christ, the coming of the Lord would not be their deliverance but their doom.

Another significant identification of the Messiah is that He is the Messenger of the covenant. This particular messianic title occurs only here, but its significance is a common messianic theme. The term "messenger" designates one who is sent on a mission with a particular work and objective to accomplish. Its association with covenant links His business to the whole redemptive plan of God. So much of God's redemptive revelation is set in terms of the covenant. Whether speaking in general terms of the covenant of grace; the essence of God's redemptive purpose; or in specific terms of the covenants with Abraham, Moses, or David, at the heart of each covenant institution is the message of God's salvific purpose in the one person of His Son. Christ is, on the one hand, the Mediator of the covenant, the Prophet, Priest, and King. On the other hand, Christ is Himself the covenant ("I the Lord have called thee…and give thee for a covenant…" [Isa. 42:6]). Christ is the fulfillment of God's promise of grace.

That the Messenger of the covenant will come suddenly to His temple answers the where and when of His coming. His coming to His temple explains why the earlier ministries of Haggai and Zechariah that inspired the completion of the temple were so crucial. Having a temple in place was a key step toward the fullness of time when Christ would come. It was, of course, Christ's coming to this temple that made it more glorious than Solomon's according to Haggai 2:7–9. That it is His temple marks Him as the rightful owner and explains His authority in His twice cleansing the temple once He came (Matt. 21:12–13; John 2:13–17). Interestingly, the word translated "suddenly" occurs about twenty-five times, usually in a context of disaster or judgment—another hint that the Messiah of their anticipation was not the real Christ. The word conveys the principal idea of something happening unexpectedly. Malachi was speaking to those who were under a sentence of judgment, and his message was simply, "Ready or not, Christ is coming."

The Purpose of Christ's Coming
Given the misconceptions of the Messiah in Malachi's day, the prophet focuses on the consequences of the wrong

notions about Christ. The Messenger who is going to come suddenly and unexpectedly to His temple comes on a mission of cleansing and judgment; He comes to purify and to punish. The images of fire and soap illustrate an aspect of the Messiah's work of judgment. As fire separates dross from the metal and as soap separates dirt from clothes, so the Messiah will do a cleansing and purifying work. In part this is the gracious solution to the questions of 3:2: "Who may abide the day of his coming? and who shall stand when he appeareth?" Only those with clean hands and pure hearts can abide the day of His coming and stand when He appears. The beauty and grace of the gospel is that Christ provides the necessary cleansing. Real metal has nothing to fear from fire, and clothes have no dread of the soap. So genuine believers should have no fear of the Lord's purifying process. It becomes the means whereby they reflect the grace of the gospel and mirror the Savior (see Eph. 5:26–27; 1 Peter 2:9).

But there is a judgment work that will be executed on the dirt and dross. Malachi 3:5 makes it clear that judgment is well earned and deserved. The prophet lists seven sins that are clear violations of God's law, the standard of judgment. This does not mean that these are the only sins that make one liable to judgment. This is an example of a literary devise called *brachylogy*, a partial list of something to designate the totality of something. The point is that all sin, not just these seven sins, deserve and earn divine punishment. The closing accusation in the verse is that they do not fear the Lord. That the Scripture so often links fearing God with knowing God suggests the ultimate, judgment-deserving sin is ignorance of God. Judgment on such sinners is the execution of justice. In their self-righteousness, they asked, "Where is the God of justice?" Woe to those who desire justice without Christ.

The Pledge of Christ's Coming

The immutability of the Lord is the guarantee that every aspect of the covenant will be fulfilled (3:6). God had a purpose for the sons of Jacob that the sins of Jacob's sons in the fifth century BC could not frustrate. God's elect will not perish; grace in Christ is greater than sin. The covenant is guaranteed. Psalm 89, the great commentary on the Davidic covenant, echoes the same theme of divine pledge (vv. 28–29, 34). In verse 34, the Lord declares that He will not alter the thing that is gone out of His lips. The word "alter" is the same word used in Malachi 3:6 to declare that God will not change. Both texts anticipate the New Testament affirmation: "For all the promises of God in him are yea, and in him Amen" (2 Cor. 1:20).

The question remains: "Who may abide the day of his coming?" (3:2). Christ came the first time, and He is certain to come again. It is imperative to repent and believe the real Christ, the Christ of God, the Christ of Scripture. The destiny of the eternal soul depends on it. So we finally come to the bottom line that I stated at the top. There is but one unchangeable answer to dead religion and every other spiritual problem: the Lord Jesus Christ.

QUESTIONS

1. Read the New Testament's narratives in Matthew 3, Mark 1, and Luke 3 about John the Baptist and note the ways in which he fulfilled the prophecy of the forerunner of Christ.

2. What evidence does Malachi give that the coming Messiah is God?

3. In what ways do the specific covenant promises to Abraham, Moses, and David focus on Christ?

4. According to Malachi, what is the twofold purpose of the Messiah's coming? What are the continuing implications and applications of that purpose?

18

The Antithesis to Dead Religion

Simply stated, the antithesis to dead religion is living religion. Although most of Malachi's message exposes deadness, he does feature aspects of living religion that stand in marked contrast to the prevalent spirit of his day. Malachi waits until he has finished his autopsy before tracking the pulse of living religion. It is directly the answer to the final incision that exposed the improper motives for serving the Lord and the stout words against Him by the religiously dead (3:13–15), but its placement in Malachi's argument overarches the entire analysis of dead religion (3:16–18). This contrast is a fitting conclusion and suggests the necessary corrective to all guilty of dead religion. His description of living religion concerns both how true worshipers see the Lord and how the Lord sees them.

The Marks of Living Religion

First, reverence is a sign of living religion: true worshipers fear the Lord (3:16). This is what the Lord deserves and demands. Remember that Malachi's second incision exposed the people's insincere worship. In 1:6 on the grounds of His being a father and a master, the Lord asked, "Where is my fear?" What was missing in the religious corpse beats in the heart of the living body. Fearing God is knowing God and living with constant awareness of Him. It includes awe, worship, respect, and the dread of displeasing the Lord. Those who truly fear the Lord recognize Him as an essential factor of life, and they live with reference to Him. The implications of fearing God—living in the reality of God—are far-reaching, touching every sphere of life. Fearing God is the foundation for true worship and the motivating directive for ethics. Religion thrives in the fear of God.

Second, meditation characterizes living religion: those who feared the Lord thought upon His name (3:16). The word for "thought" means to meditate, to regard, to take inventory. Taking inventory requires counting and listing everything that is held in stock in order to determine assets. This kind of thinking is more than a casual, routine, thoughtless devotion time; it is a conscious reckoning that God and all He is (i.e., the name, which refers to the entirety of the divine person and totality of divine perfections) is the great asset and real wealth of life. It certainly counts on Christ, who is the pearl of great price, the greatest treasure of the soul. True worship—whether private or public—is thinking time. There is an inseparable link between the head, the heart, and the hands. Right thinking about God, about Christ, and about the gospel produces right living before the Lord and in the gospel. Thinking time is never wasted time.

Third, genuine fellowship marks living religion: those who feared the Lord "spake often one to another" (3:16). This is a brief but loaded statement. Mutual communication implies mutual concern. What is implied in Malachi's terse description is what Hebrews expounds in more detail: "Let us consider one another to provoke unto love and to good works: not forsaking the assembling of ourselves together, as the manner of some is; but exhorting one another: and so much the more, as ye see the day approaching" (Heb. 10:24–25). There is an organic relationship between the work of Christ, individual salvation, and the existence of the corporate body, the church. In other words, mutual communication occurs when religion lives. Significantly as well, both Malachi and Hebrews set this mutual talking in the context of the coming Day of the Lord (3:17; 4:1). This unity of fellowship is precious and qualifies for God's special blessing (see Psalm 133).

Finally, service is a sign of living religion. Dead religion concluded that serving the Lord was unprofitable and useless (3:14). Living religion regards service as the logical expectation in the light of grace (see Rom. 12:1–2). God's discerning between those who serve Him (equated with the righteous) and those who do not (equated with the wicked) identifies living religion as an active religion (3:18). Serving is the reverse side of meditating. Remember the inseparable connection between thinking and doing. Right thinking produces right behavior. To meditate without service is religious daydreaming; to serve without meditation is heartless busywork. Meditation gives motive to service; service gives expression to meditation. Those whose religion lives will not be content just to profess their faith; they will seek to perform every duty to the glory of God. Living religion invades all the routines of life.

The Blessings of Living Religion

The blessings of living religion accrue from how the Lord sees and regards His people. The Lord always knows those who belong to Him, and He is the rewarder of all who truly seek Him (Heb. 11:6). Three special truths stand out that reveal God's genuine concern for His people. First, He carefully attends to them. Malachi declared that "the LORD hearkened, and heard it, and a book of remembrance was written before him" (3:16). God has a keen interest in His own, and He is not unmindful of those who are mindful of Him. He will always be found of those who seek Him (see 1 Chron. 28:9). Second, He claims His people as prized possessions (3:17). The word "jewels" designates a special, royal treasure. It is the word that elsewhere is translated "a peculiar treasure" (Ex. 19:5). It highlights the protected and privileged position of believers before the Lord. All the earth belongs to the Lord, but His people are special to Him. They are His jewels on display. Finally, He treats His people as family: "I will spare them, as a man spareth his own son" (3:17). The word translated "spare" conveys the idea of having and showing compassion. He protects, provides, and preserves. As members of God's family, true worshipers enjoy all the benefits of protection and provision that flow from the heavenly Father.

Malachi's description of living religion is brief and to the point, but the point is critical. The difference between dead religion and living religion is literally a matter of life and death. Not only are the contrasts evident now, but the consequences are eternal: "All that do wickedly, shall be stubble.... But unto you that fear my name shall the Sun of righteousness arise with healing in his wings" (4:1–2). Malachi ends his message with both hope and warning. In hope, he anticipates a widespread conversion through the gospel preaching of the coming Elijah-like Baptist (4:5–6). The reconciliation of families (the turning of fathers' hearts to children and children's hearts to fathers) is but a token of life-changing and life-giving transformations through the gospel of Christ. Yet in warning, his last word is the threatened curse on those who refuse the message of reconciliation. May Malachi's analysis of dead religion direct all who read it to a vital relationship with the Lord. May it, indeed, generate a genuine seeking and delight in the Messenger of the covenant, who came once and who is coming again.

QUESTIONS

1. Explain the statement that religion thrives in the fear of God.

2. What is the link between thinking and doing? In regard to the gospel, what should you be thinking, and what should you be doing?

Conclusion

It is tragic how many Christians today approach the Old Testament. They either ignore it completely or reduce it to a resource for ancient biographies that may illustrate some exemplary character trait. Or even worse, it becomes a smorgasbord of scattered and unrelated texts that are piled together as proof texts for some special interest or notion. Verses are often lifted from their contexts and thus divorced from the divinely inspired and intended meaning. My contention is that there is a relevant and modern message in the Old Testament that is discernible and discoverable. The Bible is God's special revelation, which directs sinners to Christ, guides believers in Christ, and warns against rejecting Christ. The Old Testament, including Haggai, Zechariah, and Malachi, makes a vital contribution to that message.

Malachi was the last of the postexilic prophets, and his last word was a threatened curse—not a happy way to end. But thankfully, his last word was not the last word; it was the next-to-last word. The last Word was coming. Christ, God's supreme and final Word, was on the way (see Hebrews 1).

It would be more than four hundred years before Christ would suddenly appear, and there would not be another prophetic voice during those long centuries. Interestingly, the apocryphal book of 1 Maccabees, detailing events in Israel during the second century BC, laments the cessation of prophetic activity and anticipates the coming of the next true prophet (1 Macc. 9:27; 14:41). That generation was conscious there was no new revelation. But those years of divine silence were not years of divine inactivity. For the time being, God had said all that needed to be said. Although silent, He continued His unceasing and unfailing purpose of providence to orchestrate every circumstance and event so that all would be precisely in place for the fullness of time when He would send forth His Son (Gal. 4:4) to accomplish the great work of redemption that had been the trinitarian plan from eternity.

Remarkably, the years of silence between Malachi and John the Baptist, the next prophet specifically commissioned to prepare Messiah's way, roughly equate to the years of silence between the close of Genesis and the beginning of Exodus. The narrative of Genesis ends with an expatriated family finding refuge in Egypt; Exodus begins with a multitude of people that constituted the makings of a nation. For four hundred years God was fulfilling His covenant promise to Abraham to make from him a great nation that would ultimately be the source of worldwide blessing. And then the time of redemption had come with God speaking once again. In Exodus, Israel came to birth. There had to be an Israel if there was going to be a Christ (see Rom. 9:5). And now, after four hundred years of silence again, the same covenant-keeping God would bring history to the fullness of time when the true and ideal Israel, the Christ of God, would come to birth. The time of redemption had come with God speaking once again, and this time once and for all. Nothing more would need to be said.

So during the intertestamental period, God was putting everything in place for the last word—politically, socially, religiously, and even linguistically.[5] Though there was no new revelation, what the Lord had revealed and had recorded in the Old Testament was sufficient to lead to saving faith and to keep faith vibrant. That is evident from the testimonies of Simeon and Anna, who just knew they were on the verge of the new dispensation (Luke 2:25–38). That knowledge was not just wishful thinking; it was objectively based on the Old Testament Scriptures. Significantly, they both were in the temple—the one built by Haggai's and Zechariah's congregation—when they first saw the Christ, who appeared in that temple just like Malachi said He would. The next-to-last word had pointed them to the Messiah. They knew where to look.

The messages of Haggai, Zechariah, and Malachi continue to serve the same purpose of pointing to Christ. Every old dispensation prophet did. But knowing that the messages of these three postexilic prophets would be the last word from God before Christ came in fulfillment of every redemptive promise should intensify the desire to know what they said. The next-to-last word leads directly to the last Word and is a crucial part of the context for understanding the whole conversation. The truth is timeless and universal, and I've said more than once through our survey that the God of then is the same as the God of now.

If even in a small way this study has opened up the message of these prophets by pointing to Christ and giving direction for life in the light of Christ and God's purpose for His people, I give my humble thanks to the Lord.

Notes

1. Robert Bell, *The Theological Messages of the Old Testament Books* (Greenville, S.C.: Bob Jones University Press, 2010), 451.

2. Bell, *Theological Messages*, 451–55.

3. For a synopsis of the theme of the Day of the Lord, see "The Day of the Lord," in *The Reformation Heritage KJV Study Bible* (Grand Rapids: Reformation Heritage Books, 2014), 1314.

4. For a more detailed explanation of christophanies in general and the Angel of the Lord specifically, see Michael P. V. Barrett, *Beginning at Moses: A Guide to Finding Christ in the Old Testament* (Greenville, S.C.: Ambassador-Emerald International, 1999), 145–63.

5. See *The Reformation Heritage KJV Study Bible* for a brief but helpful synopsis of what was happening between the Testaments, 1347–48.

Nov. Haggai - 3rd sermon chpt.
consider past weep,